Ten Steps TO A Federal Job

THE STARS ARE LINED UP FOR
MILITARY SPOUSES
FOR FEDERAL CAREERS

SECOND EDITION

Kathryn Troutman
with Bobbi Rossiter

The Resume Place, Inc.
Federal Career Publishers
P.O. Box 21275, Catonsville, MD 21228
Phone: 888-480-8265
www.resume-place.com
Email: resume@resume-place.com

RESUME PLACE
BUILDING CAREERS IN THE US GOVERNMENT

Printed in the United States of America
The Stars Are Lined Up for Military Spouses, Second Edition
ISBN-13: 978-1-7337779-0-2 | ISBN-10: 1-7337779-0-3
Copyright © 2019 by Kathryn Troutman

PUBLICATION TEAM
Cover Design and Interior Page Design: Brian Moore
Developmental Editing and Interior Page Layout: Paulina Chen
Military Spouse Federal Employment Consultant: Bobbi Rossiter, USMC Military Spouse
2nd Edition Military Spouse Federal Resume Contributors: Bobbi Rossiter, Jennifer Primus, Jan Meert, Nicole Becker, Natalie Goes, and Ann Johnson
2nd Edition Military Spouse Employment Advisors: Robin Sherrod, Rose Holland, Mike Kozlowski, RoseLee Bovellatangana, Stacey Delgado, and Anne Marshall
Proofreading: Pam Sikora

Table of Contents

Table of Contents

Introduction

Good news! Hiding your military spouse status on your federal resume is GONE.

This 2nd edition is dedicated to military spouses who want a federal career.

I am introducing the newest way to write a federal resume FEATURING your military spouse history and dedication to the military services. The reason that I designed this new format with military PCS history up front is because the federal government is FINALLY behind hiring spouses—more than ever! Look at the "How to Apply" section of a recent job announcement that we found:

> Applicants will be placed in one of three categories: Best Qualified, Highly Qualified, or Qualified. Within these categories, selection preference will in the following order:
>
> 1) Military Spouse preference applicants and all applicants with veterans' preference
> 2) Family Member applicants without veterans' preference
> 3) Excepted service family member applicants and Current DoDEA employees

Excerpt from a USAJOBS job announcement (School Secretary, GS-05/06) by the Department of Defense Education Activity (DODEA) in multiple locations in Europe, open 5/01/18 to 4/30/19

Five things have happened for military spouses and federal jobs since the publication of the first edition of *The Stars Are Lined Up for Military Spouses* (which was the first-ever federal resume guide for military spouses)

1. The first edition emphasized Program S (the Priority Placement Program for Military Spouses, or PPP-S), but the that program is now in flux and is either changing or going away.
   We've taken the emphasis of the book off Program S.

2. USAJOBS is advertising 70% MORE federal jobs for Military Spouses than before.
   The second edition now emphasizes USAJOBS applications.

3. Before, E.O. 13473 only applied to active duty spouses who were on PCS orders and were accompanying their spouse to the PCS location.
   Now, ANY active duty military spouse can apply for Military Spouse jobs on USAJOBS.

4. The Military Spouse Hiring Authority, E.O. 13473, used to be good only for a two-year time limit.
   Now, it is good for the entire tour at each installation.

5. There is a new (March 10, 2018) Executive Order that directs agencies to REPORT how many jobs they have posted for military spouses and how many are hired.
   This will translate into more announcements and hiring of military spouses.

IT'S TIME FOR A NEW MILITARY SPOUSE FEDERAL RESUME.

We're excited about these changes, and we hope you are too. Good luck, and write to me if you get hired into the government as a military spouse. I love success stories!

Kathryn Troutman, Author, Publisher, and former U.S. Navy Military Spouse, kathryn@resume-place.com

Ten Steps to a Federal Job®

Jobseeker's Guide

8th Edition

By Kathryn Troutman

with Paulina Chen

Ten Steps to a Federal Job® for Military and Spouses

The Stars Are Lined Up for Military Spouses is the companion guide to the *Jobseeker's Guide, Ten Steps to a Federal Job® for Military and Spouses.*

Refer to the *Jobseeker's Guide* for more in-depth information about the benefits of federal employment and how to get into government with the Resume Place's signature method: Ten Steps to a Federal Job®.

PART 01

Follow the Stars on USAJOBS® with the Military Spouse Hiring Authority

"A federal job will make me eligible for health and insurance benefits for my family and myself when my service member leaves active duty. I will have the opportunity to remain with an organization long enough to be eligible for retirement benefits."

Military spouses

If you're a military spouse, you may be eligible to apply using a non-competitive process designed to help you get a job in the federal government.

Follow the STARS for USAJOBS positions with Military Spouse Hiring Authority

 01 Learn About the Military Spouse Hiring Authority

 02 **New** Military Spouse Federal Resume

 03 How Many Jobs by the Numbers

 04 USAJOBS Military Spouse Announcements

 05 Analyze Announcements for Keywords

06 Check Off Military Spouse Boxes

 07 Add Military Spouse Documents

STAR01

What's the big deal about the Military Spouse Hiring Authority (E.O. 13473)?

If you are a U.S. citizen, you can apply for federal job announcements that are open to "the public" on USAJOBS.

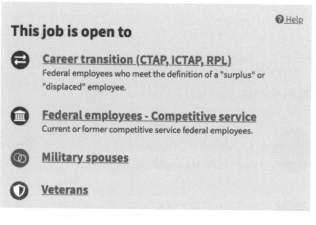

This job is open to   ❓ Help

🔄 **Career transition (CTAP, ICTAP, RPL)**
Federal employees who meet the definition of a "surplus" or "displaced" employee.

🏛 **Federal employees - Competitive service**
Current or former competitive service federal employees.

⚭ **Military spouses**

🎖 **Veterans**

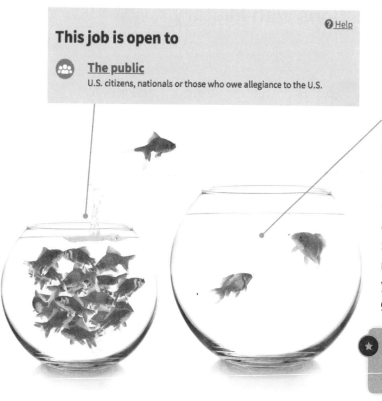

This job is open to   ❓ Help

👥 **The public**
U.S. citizens, nationals or those who owe allegiance to the U.S.

Under the Military Spouse Hiring Authority (E.O. 13473), you can also apply for announcements open to "Federal Employees - Competitive Service". This means that, as a military spouse, **more announcements are available to you, and you can apply for jobs that are limited to certain groups of people.**

⭐ *Even better, when you apply for these positions, veterans' preference does NOT apply.*

Military Spouse Hiring Authority Just Got Way Better!

The Military Spouse Hiring Authority (E.O. 13473) has undergone major changes over the last couple of years, opening up new opportunities for military spouses to apply for federal jobs.

Any Active Duty Spouse Can Use E.O. 13473. The National Defense Authorization Act for Fiscal Year 2019 made it so that any active duty spouse can leverage the hiring authority for non-competitive appointments using E.O. 13473. Yes, you read that right. This means that all military spouses are eligible to use this special hiring authority. This is major news, but it comes with a caveat: the change is temporary, lasting through the end of Fiscal Year 2023. So, take advantage now.

No Permanent Change of Station (PCS) Requirement. Bye-bye PCS, at least for now. The National Defense Authorization Act for Fiscal Year 2019 got rid of any language relating to PCS moves. Why is that exciting? This means that active duty spouses listed on their service member's orders can use E.O. 13473 regardless of branch of service and regardless of whether or not they execute a household move. This improvement also means that Activated Reservist and Guard spouses can now use this special hiring authority to support their job-seeking prospects.

Two-Year Eligibility Limitation Removed. Before, if you were a military spouse, you were limited to two-years for a non-competitive appointment subsequent to each Permanent Change of Station (PCS). The National Defense Authorization Act for Fiscal Year 2017 completely eliminated the two-year eligibility limitation for the non-competitive appointment of military spouses. This makes job searching much easier. Now, you can be appointed based on the hiring authority provided in E.O. 13473 without regard to the two-year limitation. That's a big deal for many spouses.

More Federal Agencies Are Actively Recruiting Military Spouses for Jobs. E.O. 13832, Enhancing Noncompetitive Civil Service Appointments for Military Spouses, made it a priority for federal agencies to support military spouses with more opportunities to apply for—and get—federal jobs. This E.O. made agencies accountable for reporting spouse hiring initiatives and numbers and for enhancing recruitment activities. With an annual reporting requirement, you can bet that agencies are taking this seriously.

Who Qualifies for the Military Spouse Hiring Authority?

Here are the details on the Military Spouse Hiring Authority. This current version includes many changes that have been made since E.O. 13473 was first signed in 2008.

Military Spouse Hiring Authority allows agencies to appoint a military spouse without competition. Agencies can choose to use this authority when filling competitive service positions on a temporary (not to exceed one year), term (more than one year but not more than four years), or permanent basis. The authority does not entitle spouses to an appointment over any other applicant; it is used at the discretion of the hiring agency.

You are eligible under this authority if your military spouse:

- is on active duty,
- has a 100% disability rating, OR
- died while on active duty

Based on 100% Disability: You are eligible if your active duty spouse:

- Retired under Chapter 61 of Title 10, United States Code with a 100% disability rating from the military department
- Retired or was released from active duty and has a disability rating of 100% from the Department of Veterans Affairs or the military department

There is no geographic limitation under this category. You will be required to provide documentation of your spouse's disability.

Based on Service Member's Death: If your spouse was killed while on active duty and you are not remarried, you are eligible. Similarly, there is no geographic limitation in this category., and you will be required to provide documentation of the service member's death and your marital status at the time of death.

STAR 02

Introducing the NEW military spouse federal resume

The new military spouse resume format:

1. Start with a basic federal resume
2. Add your E.O. 13473 eligibility in the resume
3. Add military spouse experience
4. Highlight your unique qualifications as a military spouse

You'll need to have a competitive federal resume in order to land a federal job in today's world. But writing a federal resume can be a daunting task for a military spouse. You may have put your career on hold or in a holding pattern to support your active duty spouse or to raise your family. You may feel like you don't have qualifications for a federal job. You may not even know where to start.

We've made things easier for you by designing a federal resume format exclusively and specifically for you, the military spouse. This format was developed based on our years of experience with writing resumes for military spouses, and HR specialists and applicants have given very positive feedback.

Because the Military Spouse is only ONE of the types of candidates for certain "competitive/federal" positions, the way to stand out is to add your Military Spouse job block. A federal employee or other candidate may not have as much experience living on and getting familiar with military bases and services as you do. You could STAND OUT if the hiring manager knows you are a military spouse and where you have lived and your experience.

How to Write Your
Military Spouse Federal Resume

01 Start with a basic federal resume

The basic federal resume is covered in the *Jobseeker's Guide* through the Ten Steps to a Federal Job. Start with creating a very rough draft of your Outline Format federal resume.

02 Add your E.O. 13473 eligibility in the resume

This step is super easy! Just add at the top of your resume: "Eligible for consideration under Executive Order 13473, September 11, 2009, Noncompetitive Appointment for Certain Military Spouses."

03 Add your military spouse experience

The military and your family have a common mission that requires certain knowledge, skill, and abilities to successfully navigate. Your experiences are assets, not drawbacks. There are two ways that you can include your military-affiliated qualifications:

- ✪ **PCS History as a Summary:** List your PCS moves and include the dates you spent at each duty station. Add a summary of the skills that made these moves successful and allowed you and your loved ones to thrive.

- ✪ **PCS History as a Job Block:** Alternatively, you could include your qualifications as a job block. Start off with a title, such as "Military Spouse Relocation Manager," "Military Spouse/Volunteer," or "Relocation Assistant." Include the dates that you've been in this position, starting with your first PCS move to your most recent. Include hours per week for this experience to count towards meeting the 52 week requirement for proving qualifications. An easy way to come up with this number is just to average the amount of time you've spent on PCS activities.

04 Highlight your unique qualifications as a military spouse

As a military spouse, you have some key qualifications you can bring out in your resume:

- ✪ You're familiar with military and government installations, procedures, policies, and regulations. Be specific and demonstrate the depth of your knowledge.

- ✪ You possess resilience as a core quality—there may be no harder job in the world than being a military spouse. Write about some of the critical problems you've solved.

- ✪ You know what it means to be mission-orientated, to deliver support, to navigate complex systems and procedures, and you have a clear sense of what it takes to adhere to timelines in a bureaucratic context. Claim credit for all of this unique, institutional knowledge.

Now take a look at an example of a military spouse federal resume on the next page to see these features in action.

See more samples in six case studies in Part 2.

Military Spouse Federal Resume Example

This is the first ever military spouse federal resume with PCS history!

Nicole Black went to the Army Community Services at Ft. Rucker, AL, in 2018. She met with Mike Kozlowski to get help with finding a job. She attended a Ten Steps to a Federal Job® workshop to get the basic step-by-step instructions for a federal application. In addition, she attended a Stars Are Lined Up for Military Spouses® workshop with Bobbi Rossiter to learn about E.O. 13473.

The Resume Place worked with Nicole on her federal resume, which initially featured her volunteer experiences at her children's schools and prior corporate experience. When Nicole asked about whether or not to include her cookie business in her federal resume, Kathryn responded with an enthusiastic, "YES!" As you will see in the resume, her entrepreneurial skills from her cookie business make her stand out.

The resulting federal resume on the following pages is targeted toward Administrative, Inventory Control, Supply Specialist, and Contact Representative positions. Nicole qualifies for these positions based on her cookie business, volunteer experience, and prior work history. Nicole is beginning her USAJOBS search now, and we will stay in touch with her results. See the full case study and more examples in Part 2 of this book.

Below: Nicole produced these stunning cookie creations of The Resume Place's logos!

NEW Military Spouse Federal Resume

NICOLE BLACK

Fort Rucker, AL 36362

(785) 555-5555 • nicoleblack77@gmail.com

MILITARY SPOUSE PREFERENCE: Spouse of Active Duty U.S. Army soldier. Eligible for consideration under Executive Order 13473, September 11, 2009, Noncompetitive Appointment for Certain Military Spouses.

> ★ EO 13473 right up front!

U.S. ARMY MILITARY SPOUSE PCS ORDER HISTORY:
- Fort Rucker, AL, U.S. Army Aviation, Mar 2018 to present
- Fort Drum, NY, 10th Mountain Division AVN, Mar 2015 to Mar 2018
- Fort Rucker, AL, U.S. Army Aviation, Jun 2012 to Mar 2015
- Fort Riley, 1st Infantry Division AVN, Feb 2007 to Jun 2012

> ★ PCS History added to the Summary at the top

SUMMARY OF SKILLS: U.S. Army Military spouse with 10+ years' experience delivering thorough and skillful administrative support to senior executives and sales teams. Adept at producing proposals, reports and letters, routing incoming mail, managing schedules, and updating and tracking documents. Effective in delivering product consultation and training. Working knowledge of PC/Mac Microsoft® Office (Word, Excel, Power Point, Outlook, Access) and Adobe software applications (Reader, Photoshop).

> ★ Summary of Skills mentions US Army Military Spouse!

PROFESSIONAL EXPERIENCE

OWNER   **03/2013 – Present**
Cookie Rookie • Fort Rucker, AL   20 hours per week

> ★ The entrepreneurial cookie business IS relevant for federal positions

Manage all operations of a home-based custom cookie decorating business, including sales, customer service, cookie design/decoration, social media communications, and billing.

CORRESPONDENCE MANAGEMENT AND CUSTOMER SERVICE: Respond to customer inquiries through text, email, or social media accounts (Instagram, Facebook, Pinterest, Messenger) to confirm quotes and pertinent order details. Manage all customer orders by verifying budget, designs, flavors, colors, and quantities. Track customer order due dates each week to ensure accuracy and avoid scheduling conflicts. Contact customers to respond to inquiries, provide order updates, or notify customer of design changes.

RESEARCH, ANALYSIS, AND PLANNING: Research and sketch out unique and creative designs by determining all background, color, overlay, and design options to render cohesive themes for customers. Stage and photograph all completed cookies. Research new products and techniques to incorporate into designs.

> ★ Outline Format with Keywords

INVENTORY CONTROL AND PROPERTY ACCOUNTABILITY: Determine best design options and meticulously organize stencils, molds, and tools required to complete orders. Evaluate

1

supply levels monthly and purchase all low stock items and special request materials (cutters, stencils, molds) through online sources.

BUDGET PLANNING AND FINANCIAL MANAGEMENT: Calculate costs of supplies and other expenses based on estimates and price lists. Track incoming revenue through PayPal and ensure expenditures are timed and within budget constraints. Confer with customers to determine appropriate theme schematics, budget, design layouts, and general order basics. Estimate order requirements and costs. Generate customer invoices and track payment daily via Excel.

COMPUTER AND SOFTWARE EXPERTISE: Utilize PicMonkey and Fotor for editing and watermarking photos and Microsoft® Word for design templates. Upload digital cookie photos to various social business accounts for marketing exposure.

KEY ACCOMPLISHMENTS:

⭐ *Accomplishments added to stand out!*

— Met corporate request by Resume Place to reproduce all of the company, book, and website logos for publication of an article and book on helping military spouses write Federal resumes. The logos were unique and intricate, and I met a tight deadline.

— Successfully delivered up to 300 cookies for school events, with 5 designs and logos and up to 5 colors total. Customers were very satisfied.

PTA VOLUNTEER   **03/2018 – Present**
Fort Rucker Primary School • Fort Rucker, AL   3 Hours per Week

ADMINISTRATIVE COORDINATOR (VOLUNTEER)   **09/2017 – 03/2018**
Parent Teacher Organization (PTO)   5 Hours per Week
West Carthage Elementary • Carthage, NY

Provided comprehensive, school-wide administrative and clerical support to the teachers and staff at an elementary school with over 400 students located near Fort Drum.

WORK PLANNING AND SCHEDULING: Assembled and packaged all program materials for students and disseminated to each class. Organized and compiled all completed classroom materials and labeled by teacher for dissemination. Ensured all shifts were covered for PTO events by cross-referencing volunteer lists.

FILE MANAGEMENT: Assisted library staff in sorting, clipping, and tracking all box top submissions. Organized and labeled library books in preparation for a new coding system.

KEY ACCOMPLISHMENTS:

⭐ *Accomplishments are interesting!*

— Contributed 100+ hours of service at various PTO events/fundraisers throughout the year, which helped the school to generate $10K.

— Spearheaded the "Helping Hands" program by providing teachers and staff weekly ongoing assistance with classroom projects, including cutting, assembling, laminating, events planning, and supervising students.

2

LEAD SALES COORDINATOR

CivicPlus • 1012 Main St., Manhattan, KS 33434

10/2007 – 05/2009

40 Hours per Week

Provided high-level administrative support for an Inc. 5000 web development company with 2,500+ local government clients nationwide. Supported four-member nationwide executive sales team. Coordinated sales support functions and customer relations.

CORRESPONDENCE MANAGEMENT: Prepared and typed final administration forms and related documents. Uploaded all new correspondence to folder on company server. Conceptualized, implemented, and conducted training on company background, procedures, forms, and FAQs for all new sales executives. Composed proposal responses and email correspondence for new clients.

REPORT PRODUCTION: Used office automation software packages and equipment to type, edit, and format letters, email responses, and responses to Request for Proposals (RFP). Reformatted templates, composed case studies of new clients, and added pictures within text to explain procedural steps. Created, maintained, and analyzed all sales forecasting/revenue spreadsheets for sales team in Microsoft® Excel. Provided monthly spreadsheets/graphs to CEO and VP Sales to make company projections and track sales.

CONTRACT REVIEW AND ANALYSIS: Identified all qualified prospective bids, determined whether requirements were feasible, and outlined response structure. Independently wrote and tailored each highly technical proposal response for appropriate government agencies and associations requesting web design/consulting services. Evaluated and printed all sales materials and proposal items weekly for team.

> ★ *Outline Format with Keywords*

KEY ACCOMPLISHMENTS:

— Promoted to Lead Coordinator in 2008 and proactively revamped the Coordinator role to ensure proper coverage of all bids. Once Coordinators were aligned and sales processes better streamlined to handle more complex bids, I implemented ongoing training on department policies and procedures for all incoming coordinators and sales executives, thus ensuring consistency of sales processes and bid guidelines.

— By conducting frequent team training and weekly discussions, as well as initiating weekly calls with assigned Sales Executives, I led my team to produce 60+ RFPs each month (up from 20), helping take the company from $2.8M to $4.5M/year.

ORDER ANALYST

Oracle (formerly NextAction) • 111 West Street, Westminster, CO

03/2006 – 07/2007

40 Hours per Week

Created, organized, and managed documents and reports in a CRM system. Worked with clients' technical staff to ensure data files were transferred and downloaded for specific product model builds. Provided model reports to key clients. Assisted sales with up-selling.

DOCUMENT MANAGEMENT: Filed and retrieved company documents and reports. Created new folders on server housing all client reports, orders, and routine requests as needed.

3

Worked with clients' technical staff to ensure necessary data files were transferred, downloaded, and used appropriately for product model builds. Provided overall model reports to key clients and assisted Sales with up-sell possibilities through reports.

KEY ACCOMPLISHMENT:
— Developed profitable relationships with clients based on excellent customer service and thorough understanding of a client's needs for a more targeted email campaign approach. Utilized internal resources across model building to ensure a 100% accurate and on-time statistical model.

SALES SUPPORT REPRESENTATIVE   **01/2001 – 02/2006**
Experian • Costa Mesa, CA   40 Hours per Week

TRAVEL MANAGEMENT: Researched rates for airfare, hotel, and car rental for all domestic travel. Created, submitted, and tracked travel arrangements and travel expense reimbursement for solo trips.

KEY ACCOMPLISHMENTS:
— Main point of contact for all credit, collections, and fraud departments for the three Top Tier banks in my area. Proactively contacted each group monthly to track concerns or training needs. Increased sales by 8% each year for each account.

— Performed sales support duties for a team of three sales representatives for a catalog marketing company that housed data on 65M+ consumers. I improved and streamlined the sales leads process by establishing an Excel-based tracking system.

CUSTOMER SERVICE MANAGER   **02/1998 – 12/2000**
Shortland Publications (McGraw-Hill) • Columbus, OH   40 Hours per Week

PROPERTY ACCOUNTABILITY: Checked inventory records to determine availability of requested merchandise before processing purchase orders. Immediately notified client by phone of any anticipated shipping delays or concerns. Alerted fulfillment staff of all large future orders to ensure inventory was available.

KEY ACCOMPLISHMENT:
— Managed more than 1,000 accounts and supported 20 sales representatives in their selling efforts. Processed all outbound and inbound orders, totaling $3M+ in revenue per year. Tracked product and inventory counts weekly through company portal and provided written updates.

EDUCATION

BACHELOR OF ARTS (B.A.), 1998
Adams State University • Alamosa, CO • GPA: 3.20/4.00
— Major: Exercise Physiology & Leisure Sciences / K-12 Education
— Minor: Business

4

STAR03

How many jobs are available in the federal government for military spouses?

Because military spouses often live on or near base, it's important to know how many jobs there are on military bases that you could apply to. You have dedicated your life, time, and family to living on military bases—so, why not work there too?

To find where the jobs are, take some time to do some research. Here are a few key tips:

- ✪ **Tip #1:** Look at the numbers of General Schedule (GS) and Non-Appropriated Funding (NAF) jobs on military bases in the U.S. The larger bases typically have more opportunities, but you really want to target GS or NAF positions.

- ✪ **Tip #2:** Take a look at the annually compiled list of the Best Places to Work in the Federal Government. This list shows what agencies do the best jobs at keeping their employees happy, as rated by the employees themselves. Many of these agencies support military functions, and there could be job opportunities for you.

- ✪ **Tip #3:** Research the agencies that are hiring the most. This gives you a sense of which agencies are hiring the most people so that you can better manage your job search campaign. You want to know where the jobs are.

- ✪ **Tip #4:** You also need to know what jobs are available. So what are the top job titles in federal hiring? Understanding this will create a clear picture of what types of positions agencies most routinely are trying to fill.

With this information you can plan your federal job search by your next installation, the job title, and agency. The more carefully you apply this information, the better your odds of landing a federal job.

Jobs on Military Bases

The table below and on the following pages shows the number of DOD Appropriated Fund (APF) and Non-Appropriated Fund (NAF) Civilians by installation as of November 2017. This list includes the installations with at least 100 total individuals.

Installation	APF	NAF	Total
* 1ST MARINE CORPS DISTRICT	138	0	138
ABERDEEN PROVING GROUND	105	58	163
ALBANY MCLB	158	0	158
ANDREWS AFB	136	298	434
ANNAPOLIS NS (INCL USNA)	124	0	124
ANNISTON ARMY DEPOT	249	0	249
BARKSDALE AFB	75	182	257
BATTLE CREEK FEDERAL CENTER	1244	16	1260
BEALE AFB	37	80	117
BEAUFORT MCAS	205	0	205
BUCKLEY AFB	292	0	292
CAMP LEJEUNE MCB	682	0	682
CAMP PENDLETON	169	0	169
CANNON AFB	32	92	124
CHARLESTON AFB	70	89	159
CHERRY POINT MCAS	287	0	287
CORONADO NAV AMPHIB BASE	107	0	107
CORPUS CHRISTI NAS	105	0	105
DAVIS-MONTHAN AFB	399	198	597
DEF DISTRIBUTION CTR-SAN JOAQU	1244	57	1301
DEFENSE DIST DEPOT SUSQUEHANNA	2911	156	3067
DEFENSE SUPPLY CTR PHILA	3119	0	3119
DFAS CLEVELAND CENTER	2282	0	2282
DFAS COLUMBUS CENTER	6130	0	6130
DFAS INDIANAPOLIS CENTER	4297	0	4297
DISA HQTRS	750	0	750
DOD CENTER MONTEREY/FORT ORD	212	85	297
DOVER AFB	105	55	160
DYESS AFB	38	99	137
EDWARDS AFB	51	134	185
EGLIN AFB	187	334	521
ELECTRONICS CTR - DAYTON	0	206	206
ELMENDORF AFB	109	267	376
ENDIST LITTLE ROCK AR	0	190	190

Installation	APF	NAF	Total
ENDIST LOS ANGELES CA	170	74	244
FAIRCHILD AFB	52	101	153
FORT BELVOIR	5454	581	6035
FORT BENNING	701	0	701
FORT BLISS	181	695	876
FORT BRAGG	1225	954	2179
FORT CAMPBELL	455	547	1002
FORT CARSON	407	489	896
FORT DETRICK	102	0	102
FORT DIX	16	233	249
FORT DRUM	91	335	426
FORT EUSTIS	122	205	327
FORT GEORGE G. MEADE	3604	187	3791
FORT GORDON	118	361	479
FORT HAMILTON	41	68	109
FORT HOOD	258	767	1025
FORT HUACHUCA	292	206	498
FORT IRWIN	152	314	466
FORT JACKSON	256	295	551
FORT JONATHAN WAINWRIGHT	77	75	152
FORT KNOX	478	299	777
FORT LEAVENWORTH	70	156	226
FORT LEE	1319	319	1638
FORT LEONARD WOOD	109	409	518
FORT LESLIE J MCNAIR	442	0	442
FORT LEWIS	243	715	958
FORT MONROE	148	0	148
FORT MYER	181	98	279
FORT POLK	86	228	314
FORT RICHIE	0	138	138
FORT RILEY	132	0	132
FORT RUCKER	234	153	387
FORT SAM HOUSTON	870	482	1352
FORT SHAFTER	102	0	102
FORT SILL	134	339	473

Jobs on Military Bases continued

Installation	APF	NAF	Total
FORT STEWART	411	53	464
FORT WORTH USARC	558	165	723
HANSCOM AFB	43	84	127
HILL AFB	805	161	966
HOLLOMAN AFB	45	100	145
HURLBURT FIELD	63	65	128
JACKSONVILLE NAS	344	0	344
JOINT BASE ANACOSTIA-BOLLING	308	106	414
KEESLER AFB	78	239	317
KELLY AFB	117	0	117
KIRTLAND AFB	287	124	411
LACKLAND AFB	516	570	1086
LANGLEY AFB	132	213	345
LETTERKENNY ARMY DEPOT	278	0	278
LORING AFB	602	0	602
LOS ANGELES AFB	260	0	260
LUKE AFB	91	202	293
LYNDON B. JOHNSON SPACE CTR	168	0	168
MACDILL AFB	201	229	430
MALMSTROM AFB	45	78	123
MARCH AFB	134	55	189
MAXWELL AFB (INCL. GUNTER)	461	200	661
MCAS MIRAMAR	112	0	112
MCCDC QUANTICO VA	675	0	675
MCCHORD AFB	114	181	295
MCCLELLAN AFB	351	73	424
MCCONNELL AFB	115	46	161
MCGUIRE AFB	102	0	102
MICHIGAM ARMY MISSILE PLANT	148	0	148
MINOT AFB	44	121	165
MOUNTAIN HOME AFB	40	112	152
NAVAL BASE KITSAP-BANGOR	110	0	110
NAVAL BASE KITSAP-BREMERTON	272	0	272
NAVAL BASE PEARL HARBOR	645	0	645
NAVAL STATION GREAT LAKES	128	0	128
NAVCAMS E. PACIFIC	139	0	139
NAVSURFWEAPCEN DAHLGREN	234	0	234
NAVY RECRUITING AREA 7 DALLAS	196	0	196

Installation	APF	NAF	Total
NAVY RECRUITING AREA THREE	185	0	185
NELLIC AFB	115	0	115
NEW LONDON NAVSUBBASE	106	0	106
NNMC BETHESDA	3113	0	3113
NORFOLK NAVAL BASE	817	0	817
OCEANA NAS	242	0	242
OFFUTT AFB	98	145	243
ONIZUKA AFB	139	0	139
PATRICK AFB	110	148	258
PENSACOLA NAS	185	0	185
PENTAGON	3278	0	3278
PETERSON AFB	172	130	302
PHOENIX AGS	161	0	161
PORT HUENEME NCBC	148	0	148
RANDOLPH AFB	113	275	388
RED RIVER DEPOT	649	45	694
REDSTONE ARSENAL	2427	181	2608
RICHMOND DEF DEPOT	2708	50	2758
ROBINS AFB	866	180	1046
SALT LAKE CITY IAP AGS	106	0	106
SAN DIEGO NAVSTA	684	0	684
SCHOFIELD BARRACKS	0	489	489
SCOTT AFB	749	203	952
SEYMOUR JOHNSON AFB	54	57	111
SHAW AFB	53	116	169
SHEPPARD AFB	55	150	205
STRATFORD ARMY ENGINE PLANT	158	0	158
TINKER AFB	1532	241	1773
TRAVIS AFB	200	336	536
TYNDALL AFB	60	111	171
USAF ACADEMY	71	84	155
VANDENBERG AFB	69	80	149
WASHINGTON NAVDIST HQ	2386	0	2386
WEST POINT MILRES	219	128	347
WHITEMAN AFB	49	82	131
WRIGHT-PATTERSON AFB	518	213	731
YORKTOWN NAVWEAPSTA	53	759	812

Updates will be posted regularly on www.resume-place.com.

Top Agency Hires

Agency	Oct–Dec 2016	Jan–Mar 2017	Apr–Jun 2017	Jul–Sep 2017	FY 2017
Agency - All	47408	40690	56361	44905	189364
CABINET LEVEL AGENCIES	45289	38093	54858	40357	178597
Department of Veterans Affairs	9585	8611	9755	12355	40306
Department of Homeland Security	5994	4485	4370	6342	21191
Department of the Army	5450	3154	5703	5074	19381
Department of Agriculture	2027	2461	12033	1295	17816
Department of the Interior	1599	2104	7125	1238	12066
Department of the Air Force	3763	2261	3087	2672	11783
Department of the Navy	2874	1846	3206	3518	11444
Department of Defense	3233	1766	2190	2925	10114
LARGE INDEPENDENT AGENCIES (1000 OR MORE EMPLOYEES)	1798	2137	1219	4290	9444
Department of the Treasury	3123	4316	688	160	8287
Department of Justice	1822	1729	1746	1461	6758
Department of Health and Human Services	2256	1743	1366	1299	6664
Department of Commerce	1593	1660	2295	946	6494
Department of Transportation	1018	1001	930	748	3697
Social Security Administration	104	51	371	1840	2366
Small Business Administration	308	99	24	1564	1995
MEDIUM INDEPENDENT AGENCIES (100-999 EMPLOYEES)	278	378	233	208	1097
National Aeronautics and Space Administration	130	470	66	171	837
Environmental Protection Agency	253	433	75	38	799
Department of Energy	207	242	212	109	770
Department of State	283	225	68	79	655
General Services Administration	254	189	127	77	647
Department of Labor	226	281	23	40	570
Office of Personnel Management	107	147	68	133	455
Department of Housing and Urban Development	137	123	35	78	373
Federal Deposit Insurance Corporation	22	50	170	109	351
Smithsonian Institution	119	125	42	63	349
Department of Education	99	85	26	18	228
SMALL INDEPENDENT AGENCIES (LESS THAN 100 EMPLOYEES)	43	82	51	50	226
National Science Foundation	71	57	38	46	212
National Archives and Records Administration	62	69	7	65	203
Peace Corps	74	63	27	20	184
Federal Reserve System	23	75	59	15	172
Securities and Exchange Commission	79	49	12	11	151
Agency for International Development	42	58	16	27	143
Federal Trade Commission	19	29	56	30	134
Office of Management And Budget	28	45	26	31	130
Corporation for National and Community Service	30	54	8	17	109
Equal Employment Opportunity Commission	38	51	0	3	92
Federal Housing Finance Agency	9	8	48	10	75
Consumer Product Safety Commission	18	9	44	1	72
National Labor Relations Board	17	31	4	13	65
Broadcasting Board of Governors	14	35	3	11.	63
Federal Communications Commission	17	17	7	20	61
Government Printing Office	13	13	22	11	59
Pension Benefit Guaranty Corporation	22	31	0	3	56
National Foundation on the Arts and the Humanities	16	20	4	15	55

Research by The Resume Place. Updates will be posted regularly at www.resume-place.com.

Best Places to Work 2018

Rank	Agency	2018	2017	Change (2017–18)
LARGE AGENCIES				
1	National Aeronautics and Space Administration	81.2	80.9	0.3
2	Department of Health and Human Services	70.9	70.4	0.5
3	Department of Commerce	70.3	69.2	1.1
4	Department of Transportation	67.7	67.6	0.1
5	Intelligence Community	66.3	66.6	-0.3
6	Department of Veterans Affairs	64.2		
7	Department of the Navy	63.2	63.8	-0.6
7	Office of the Secretary of Defense, Joint Staff, Defense Agencies, and Department of Defense Field Activities	63.2	61.1	2.1
9	Department of the Interior	62.8	63.9	-1.1
10	Department of Justice	62.6	63.7	-1.1
MIDSIZE AGENCIES				
1	Federal Trade Commission	84	81.4	2.6
2	Federal Energy Regulatory Commission	83.9	82.9	1.0
3	Securities and Exchange Commission	82.1	80.9	1.2
4	Government Accountability Office	80.7	82.5	-1.8
5	Federal Deposit Insurance Corporation	80.5	81.9	-1.4
6	Peace Corps	79.8	80.7	-0.9
7	Smithsonian Institution	76.7	76.9	-0.2
8	National Science Foundation	75.5	74.7	0.8
9	Architect of the Capitol	75.3		
10	General Services Administration	74.5	73.7	0.8
SMALL AGENCIES				
1	Federal Mediation and Conciliation Service	87.2	86.9	0.3
2	U.S. International Trade Commission	85.7	80.9	4.8
3	Congressional Budget Office	85.3		
4	Farm Credit Administration	81.1	80.5	0.6
5	Pension Benefit Guaranty Corporation	78.3	73.5	4.8
6	National Transportation Safety Board	77.8	77.5	0.3
7	Office of Management and Budget	75	75.4	-0.4
8	National Endowment for the Humanities	74.9	71.4	3.5
9	Federal Maritime Commission	74.4	67.5	6.9
10	Overseas Private Investment Corporation	73.6	79.8	-6.2

Source: Partnership for Public Service, Best Places to Work, www.ourpublicservice.org

Top 30 Job Titles in the Federal Government

Only jobs with an asterisk (*) require a degree or specific education.

Job Title (Series Number)	Number of U.S. employees
Miscellaneous Administration and Program (0301)	97,786
Nurse (0610)*	83,985
Information Technology Management (2210)	82,399
Management and Program Analysis (0343)	73,507
Miscellaneous Clerk and Assistant (0303)	55,851
Compliance Inspection and Support (1802)	51,486
Criminal Investigation (1811)	43,351
General Inspection, Investigation, Enforcement, and Compliance Series (1801)	37,973
General Attorney (0905)*	37,876
Contracting (1102)*	37,208
Medical Officer (0602)*	34,468
Human Resources Management (0201)	29,284
Medical Support Assistance (0679)	28,667
Social Insurance Administration (0105)	27,569
General Business and Industry (1101)	26,575
General Engineering (0801)*	26,280
Financial Administration and Program (0501)	25,410
Contact Representative (0962)	25,259
Customs and Border Protection (1895)	23,017
General Natural Resources Management and Biological Sciences (0401)	20,989
Air Traffic Control (2152)	20,298
Logistics Management (0346)	19,399
Border Patrol Enforcement Series (1896)	19,364
Electronics Engineering (0855)	18,810
Practical Nurse (0620)	18,621
Correctional Officer (0007)	18,177
Social Work (0185)	16,504
Forestry Technician (0462)	15,876
General Health Science (0601)	15,202

Research by The Resume Place.
Updates will be posted regularly at www.resume-place.com.

USAJOBS
MILITARY SPOUSE ANNOUNCEMENTS

President Trump surprised us with E.O. 13832, a directive mandating that agencies prioritize military spouse hiring, enhance recruitment of military spouses, and annual report on their military spouse initiatives and numbers hired. This is exciting because we're already seeing more military spouse listing on USAJOBS than ever.

Since the Executive Order was issued, researchers at the Resume Place have been tracking the number of military spouse positions posted on USAJOBS. Guess what? We're thrilled to report that the order is having the intended effect: more military spouse jobs! In fact, a comparative analysis shows that since the issuance of the order, there's been a **900%** increase in posted jobs. That's a big deal!

INSTALLATION	October 2017			December 2018		
	Competitive Service Openings	Mil Spouse Openings	% of Mil Jobs	Competitive Service Openings	Mil Spouse Openings	% of Mil Jobs
WRIGHT-PATTERSON AFB, OH	201	8	3.98%	71	55	77.46%
BUCKLEY AFB, CO	67	0	0.00%	84	51	60.71%
FORT LEAVENWORTH, KS	12	2	16.67%	61	42	68.85%
JOINT BASE LEWIS-MCCORD, WA	37	2	5.41%	52	33	63.46%
NELLIS AFB, NV	95	1	1.05%	62	32	51.61%
ELMENDORF AFB	131	13	9.92%	44	30	68.18%
FORT SILL, OK	34	2	5.88%	30	30	100.00%
OFFUTT AFB, NE	117	2	1.71%	38	27	71.05%
FORT HOOD, TX	45	15	33.33%	35	26	74.29%
FORT DEVENS, MA	23	4	17.39%	35	24	68.57%
FORT KNOX, KY	31	8	25.81%	21	23	109.52%
SHAW AFB, SC	34	1	2.94%	39	23	58.97%
FORT LEE, VA	28	6	21.43%	37	22	59.46%
MAXWELL AFB, AL	109	3	2.75%	30	22	73.33%
FORT LEONARDWOOD, MO	33	12	36.36%	23	21	91.30%
TOTALS (ALL, including Installations not shown)	2434	166	**6.82%**	1179	728	**61.75%**

Notes: Research by Jan Meert/Resume Place. Updates will be posted regularly at www.resume-place.com.

Find USAJOBS Announcements

Finding a good USAJOBS announcement that matches your location, salary level, and qualifications is easy for military spouses. Here is our recommended way to start:

Search USAJOBS with these starter search categories:

- ✪ Military Spouse positions
- ✪ Geographic region
- ✪ Salary range

Human Resources Assistant (Military)
U.S. Army Training and Doctrine Command
Department of the Army
Multiple Locations

Starting at $41,365 (GS 7)
30 Sep 2021 • Full-Time

🕓 *Open 01/02/2019 to 12/31/2019*

Supply Technician (Motor Vehicle Operator)
U.S. Army Training and Doctrine Command
Department of the Army
Multiple Locations

Starting at $41,365 (GS 7)
30 Sep 2021 • Full-Time

🕓 *Open 01/02/2019 to 12/31/2019*

Program Assistant (Military)
U.S. Army Training and Doctrine Command
Department of the Army
Multiple Locations

Starting at $41,365 (GS 7)
30 Sep 2021 • Full-Time

🕓 *Open 01/02/2019 to 12/31/2019*

ADMINISTRATIVE/TECHNICAL SPECIALIST
Naval Sea Systems Command
Department of the Navy
Multiple Locations

Starting at $50,912 (NT 3-4)
Permanent • Full-Time

🕓 *Open 01/04/2019 to 01/03/2020*

Program Specialist
Board of Veterans Appeals
Department of Veterans Affairs
📍 Washington, District of Columbia

Starting at $45,972 (GS 7)
Permanent • Full-Time

🕓 *Open 01/10/2019 to 02/01/2019*

Identify Military Spouse Jobs in USAJOBS
Which USAJOBS announcements qualify?

Four types of federal announcements for Military Spouses:

Open to the public
Military Spouse Hiring Authority does not apply, but you can apply for these positions.

Competitive service
Some of these positions allow spouses to apply. You will see the Military Spouse widget in the announcement.

Excepted service
Some of these positions allow spouses to apply. You will see the Military Spouse widget in the announcement.

Military spouses
ALL of these announcements are available to spouses who are authorized by E.O. 13473, Military Spouse Hiring Authority.

More military spouse jobs will be added soon!

Top filters	More filters

Hiring path   ❓ Help

Select all

- ☑ 👥 Open to the public (1771)

Federal employees (1915)
- ☑ 🏛 Competitive service (462)
- ☑ 🏛 Excepted service (382)
- ☐ ◎ Internal to an agency (688)
- ☐ ⇄ Career transition (CTAP, ICTAP, RPL) (325)
- ☐ 🌲 Land & base management (58)

Armed forces (693)
- ☐ 🛡 Veterans (456)
- ☑ ◎ Military spouses (172)
- ☐ 🚩 National Guard & Reserves (65)

Students & recent graduates (30)
- ☐ 📖 Students (19)
- ☐ 🎓 Recent graduates (11)

Senior executives (59)
- ☐ 💼 Senior executives (59)

Additional paths (432)
- ☐ ♿ Individuals with disabilities (200)
- ☐ ✈ Family of overseas employees (57)
- ☐ ⚙ Native Americans (18)
- ☐ 🌐 Peace Corps & AmeriCorps Vista (73)
- ☐ ✳ Special authorities (84)

Veterans' Preference and Military Spouse Announcements

Military spouse USAJOBS announcements WILL NOT apply Veterans' Preference.

? Help

This job is open to

⇄ **Career transition (CTAP, ICTAP, RPL)**
Federal employees who meet the definition of a "surplus" or "displaced" employee.

🏛 **Federal employees - Competitive service**
Current or former competitive service federal employees.

◎ **Military spouses**

◗ **Veterans**

Open to the Public announcements WILL APPLY Veterans' Preference.

Open to the public ✕

✖ Remove all filters

Viewing 1 – 10 of 1771 jobs   Sort by Relevance ⬍

🔖 Save this search. We'll email you new jobs as they become available.

Human Resources Specialist (NAF/Strategic Response) NF 04
US Army Civilian Human Resources Agency
Department of the Army
Multiple Locations

Starting at $55,000 (NF 4)
Permanent • Full-Time

🕐 Open 01/31/2019 to 02/13/2019

HR ASST
Army National Guard Units
Department of the Army
📍 Camp Murray, Washington

Starting at $36,213 (GS 5)
Indefinite, Excepted Service • Full-Time

🕐 Open 01/23/2019 to 02/07/2019

👤 Sign in to use your profile.

Top filters   **More filters**

Hiring path   ? Help
Select all

☑ ◎ Open to the public (1771)

Federal employees (1915)
☐ 🏛 Competitive service (462)
☐ 🏛 Excepted service (382)
☐ ◎ Internal to an agency (688)
☐ ⇄ Career transition (CTAP, ICTAP, RPL) (325)
☐ 🌲 Land & base management (58)

Armed forces (693)
☐ ◗ Veterans (456)
☐ ◎ Military spouses (172)

Save a Search for Job Matches at Your Installation

Saving your searches will help you easily find announcements that are similar to the ones you've already found. New announcements will be automatically emailed to you, on a frequency you specify, saving you a lot of time.

To save a search, sign into your USAJOBS account. Start a job search by entering a keyword or location in the search box and click SEARCH. Narrow your results with the filters and then click the "Save this search" link. Be sure to give your search a meaningful name as it will be in the subject line of the email that comes to your inbox.

STAR 05

Back to the basics here with keywords

Star 5 applies to every federal job application, including Military Spouses. If your resume doesn't match the job announcement, you likely won't be rated as Best Qualified. The human resources specialist will review your federal resume and look for the keywords from the Specialized Experience, Qualifications, KSAs, competencies, questionnaire, and throughout the announcement. Finding the keywords and adding them to your federal resume is crucial.

We selected popular jobs that military spouses might find on military bases to GIVE you the keywords. Study this list and add these keywords into your brand new Outline Format federal resume. You will find that your federal resume will get better results if you change the keywords to match each announcement.

Analyze Announcements

To make a list of keywords for your federal resume, you will need to analyze the Responsibilities, Requirements, Specialized Experiences, KSAs and Competencies in the announcement.

Exercise
Circle the keywords in the following sections.

Office Automation Assistant

DEPARTMENT OF DEFENSE
Department of Defense Education Activity
DoDEA Europe South District

Responsibilities: Circle the keywords

Responsibilities

Performs various office automation duties in support of school administration.

Uses database and spreadsheet software to enter, revise, sort and retrieve data pertaining to school administration.

Serves as back-up and assists the School Information Assistant by entering and retrieving information in the Student Management System (SMS) database.

Assists in the registration of new students.

Prepares and tracks Military Interdepartmental Purchase requests (MIPRs) and provides printouts of available funds information to the school principal.

Orders, maintains, and displays controlling regulations, publications and required forms that may have been issued by a variety of sources. May perform office automation work, including word processing, and a variety of clerical functions in support of a special education assessor office within the Department of Defense Education Activity (DoDEA) at a school or school complex level.

★ *Example keywords. Find more!*

Qualifications: Circle the keywords

In order to qualify for this position, you need one year of specialized experience at the GS-04 level. Examples of specialized experience include: using a personal computer and multiple functions of a variety of software types (e.g., word processing, spreadsheets, databases, graphics) to prepare a variety of letters, messages, memoranda, reports, statistical material, graphics, school bulletins, parent newsletters, faculty and parent handbooks, and other documents from oral instructions, hand-written rough drafts, or voice recordings; assisting in registration of incoming students; establishing and managing all files; and/or orders and maintains supplies and materials.

Typing Proficiency Requirements: In addition to meeting the experience and/or education requirements, applicants must include a certificate of proficiency or self-certify that they can type at least 40 words per minute. Your resume must support your self-certification of your typing ability. Otherwise you may not meet the minimum qualifications requirements for this position.

WORK/LIFE SPECIALIST

DEPARTMENT OF THE AIR FORCE
Headquarters, Air Force Space Command

Specialized Experience: Circle the keywords

SPECIALIZED EXPERIENCE: One year of specialized experience for GS-0101-09 which includes thorough knowledge of social services delivery systems and concepts, principles, and theories relating to one or more of the social or behavioral science fields to assess needs and concerns of clients and help them to understand how certain behavior patterns/attitudes impact and affect their career, transition, relocation, and family situation and learn about their abilities, capacities, interests, and goals concerning their various work/life requirements. This definition of specialized experience is typical of work performed at the GS-07 grade/level or equivalent in the federal service.

OR EDUCATION: Master's or equivalent graduate degree or 2 full years of progressively higher level graduate education leading to such a degree in a field which demonstrates the knowledge, skills, and abilities necessary to do the work of the position, such as: behavioral or social science; or related disciplines appropriate to the position. NOTE: YOU MUST SUBMIT COPIES OF YOUR OFFICIAL TRANSCRIPTS.

Knowledge, Skills, and Abilities (KSAs): Circle the keywords

KNOWLEDGE, SKILLS AND ABILITIES (KSAs): Your qualifications will be evaluated on the basis of your level of knowledge, skills, abilities and/or competencies in the following areas:

1. Knowledge of social services delivery systems as well as concepts, principles, theories, and practices relating to one or more of the social or behavioral science fields.

2. Knowledge of personal financial management practices and techniques to provide clients with appropriate financial data and practical financial skills to enable them to make informed personal financial management decisions.

3. Skill in conducting interviews to establish the nature and extent of concerns/issues, provide assistance in developing goals and plans, and determine appropriate referral services/options.

4. Skill in establishing and maintaining effective working relationships using tact and diplomacy in interactions with individuals/families and with program representatives and officials.

5. Ability to communicate effectively both orally and in writing.

Questionnaire: Circle the keywords

Program Analyst
DEPARTMENT OF ENERGY
National Nuclear Security Administration

2 Which of the following tasks have you performed as a regular part of your job (check all that apply)?

(Gather data,) interpret and apply guidelines and policy, and analyze information to reach conclusions.

Develop and implement technically feasible and (cost effective strategies) to solve complex issues or problems.

Analyze complex issues, identify problems, evaluate alternatives, and develop solutions.

Organize, analyze, and facilitate the implementation and documentation of policies and programs.

Explain policy or procedures to other staff members.

None of the above.

3 Please tell us where in your resume the experience you claimed in the above response is reflected. Include only time frame(s) and title of the position(s). If experience is Federal Civilian include only time frame(s) and title/series/grade. (Maximum length of 250 characters.)

4 Skill evaluating and analyzing data and developing metrics in order to assist in assessing and documenting the progress of activities and/or programs. Select the ONE option that best describes your experience.

I have assisted in the evaluation and analysis of data and development of metrics to measure the progress of an activity and/or programs (for example: records management, security, property management, budget) against organizational goals and report the results.

I have assisted in the evaluation and analysis of data and development of metrics to measure an activity against organizational goals for major support program.

I have evaluated and analyzed data and developed metrics to measure the progress of internal office procedures and processes.

I do not have related experience.

5 Please tell us where in your resume the experience you claimed in the above response is reflected. Include only time frame(s) and title of the position(s). If experience is Federal Civilian include only time frame(s) and title/series/grade. (Maximum length of 250 characters.)

6 Skill measuring the adequacy and effectiveness of programs in order to make recommendations for program improvement. Select the ONE option that best describes your experience.

I have utilized analytical and evaluative methods, tools, and techniques in order to assist in the development and conduct of studies to assess the efficiency/effectiveness of programs (for example: records management, security, property management, budget) in order to assess needs and develop recruitment strategies to meet program objectives.

I have utilized analytical and evaluative methods, tools, and techniques in order to assist in the development and conduct of studies to assess the efficiency/effectiveness for a major support program.

I have utilized analytical and evaluative methods, tools, and techniques in order to conduct studies to assess the efficiency/effectiveness of internal office procedures and processes.

I do not have related experience.

Make a List of Keywords and Match Your Federal Resume to the Announcement

Start making your list of keywords from the vacancy announcement and use these keywords in your resume.

Personnel Security Specialist

DEPARTMENT OF JUSTICE
Executive Office for U.S. Attorneys and the Office of the U.S. Attorneys

Qualifications

GS-9: To be eligible at the **GS-9** level, you must meet **ONE** full year of specialized experience equivalent to the GS-7 level as defined below:

Experience applying knowledge of laws, regulations, Executive Orders, and/or agency and office procedures related to personnel security programs.

Experience reviewing background information, credit information/reports, and criminal records checks to determine suitability for security clearances.

Experience using automated databases to track information and generate reports.

You will be rated on the following Competencies:

- Technical Competence
- Customer Service
- Information Management
- Oral Communication
- Attention to Detail

KEYWORDS FOR YOUR FEDERAL RESUME TO MATCH THIS ANNOUNCEMENT

- POLICIES AND PROCEDURES ON PERSONNEL SECURITY PROGRAMS
- REVIEW BACKGROUND INFORMATION
- REVIEW CREDIT INFORMATION AND CRIMINAL RECORDS
- USE AUTOMATED DATABASES
- GENERATE REPORTS
- CUSTOMER SERVICE
- INFORMATION MANAGEMENT

HOW TO MATCH YOUR FEDERAL RESUME TO GET BEST QUALIFIED

1. Your resume must show the One Year Specialized Experience.
2. Your federal resume must match keywords.
3. Your resume must include the education that is required.
4. The questionnaire has to be answered at least 90% perfect.
5. Required documents must be included.
6. Your resume must be compliant with required information, as in the USAJOBS Builder.

Keywords for Popular Job Series for Military Spouses

The human resources specialist needs to see certain knowledge, skills, and abilities in your resume, and those can be demonstrated by specific keywords relating to a series. Job series keywords are listed in the **classification standards** or in related job announcements. In the chart below, we have extracted sample keyword lists for common occupational series that a military spouse might be trying to qualify for. Use these keywords in your resume if you can.

If you apply to any of these positions, use these keywords as HEADLINES in your federal resume. For example, HEADLINE KEYWORDS for Social Services, Employee Assistance:

INTERPRET REGULATIONS

ASSESS CLIENTS AND DETERMINE SERVICES

NEGOTIATE AGREEMENTS

REVIEW MEDICAL AND EDUCATIONAL FORMS

ASSIST CUSTOMERS

Series	Series Title	Title	Keywords
101	Social Services	Employee Assistance Program Coordinator	Interpret regulations, policies Assess clients and determine services Develop and delivery training related to EAP Negotiate agreements to correct EAP inadequacies Knowledge of EAP programs Knowledge of EAP requirements Administrative Communications Review medical and educational forms Electronic medical records systems Complete medical and educational forms Assist customers with identifying programs/services
101	Social Services	Family Advocacy Program	Domestic abuse victim advocacy Child advocacy Working with non-offending parent Child abuse and domestic abuse Crisis intervention Safety planning and procedures Civilian and military orders of protection Dynamics of domestic, interpersonal, and family violence Knowledge of community services Laws of family relationships Prepare court testimony Crisis situations Oral communications
101	Social Services	Victim Advocate	Administrative duties Victim advocacy services Victim support services Administrative duties Advocacy services to victims or survivors of sexual assault and sexual harassment Conduct assessments with clients Evaluate needs and risks Recognize need for professional intervention Refer to appropriate services Maintain partnerships with community Conduct training / seminars

Series	Series Title	Title	Keywords
101, 301, 303	Social Services, Program Analysis, Miscellaneous Clerk and Assistant	Sexual Assault Response Coordinator	Four year degree in behavior health and social science Experience with victims of sexual assault or victim advocacy service Knowledge of DOD SAPR Knowledge of local, state, and federal laws and military regulations Training and briefings Program development plans Sensitivity and empathy for victims Build trust with socially-diverse victims and families Analytical skills for crisis situations Work cooperatively with military and civilian legal and medical institutions Written and oral communications skills Data collection and management report production
201 & 203	Human Resources Management/Assistance	Staffing	Conduct job analysis Create occupational questionnaires and vacancy announcements Determine qualifications to develop a referral list Research civilian personnel regulations Resolve staffing issues Automated staffing tools Fundamental classification and position management laws Civilian HR classification and processes
301	Miscellaneous Administration and Program	Analysis and Planning	Identify potential benefits / uses of automation Improve efficiency of administrative support Research new or improved business practices Process and audit data files for work operations Analyze and evaluate (quantitative or qualitative basis) Develop procedures to improve control systems Research new or improved business practices
301	Misc Admin and Program Management, Misc Clerk and Assistant	Training-Education	Knowledge of financial or budget transactions Knowledge of budget or financial regulations Ability to resolve complaints or discrepancies Advise on training programs / procedures Knowledge of education and training policies Processes for on-the-job, career development classes Knowledge of personnel data system Process training and education transactions Knowledge of staff functions for customer services
343	Management and Program Analyst	Systems Acquisition	Quality of products or services Quality control, procurement, inspection, production Contracting and purchasing Supply and storage Industrial and production planning Research and engineering Maintenance Testing and evaluation Review production activities and capabilities Analyze quality data to detect unsatisfactory trends Investigate customer complaints and deficiency reports Read, interpret and apply technical data Review and evaluate supply systems operations

★ *If you apply to these positions, these keywords are critical to get BEST QUALIFIED.*

Series	Series Title	Title	Keywords
640	Health Aid & Technician	Nutrition	Control patient meal orders Update room service menus Provide food, nutrition and/or dietetics services Respond to calls, patient services Computerized systems for medical care Communications skills Teamwork
1102	Contract and Procurement	Contract Administrator	Negotiate contract prices and terms Review contract proposals Draft contract specifications Contract administration principles Administer a group of contracts Negotiation techniques during pre-post award Price and cost analysis Monitor contractor performance to ensure compliance with contractual requirements
1702	General Education and Training	Education Services	Education theories, principles of secondary or adult education Knowledge of standardized military personnel rules Counsel on military careers Military personnel testing on careers Knowledge of career development and training concepts Knowledge of college degrees, curriculum Regulations for destruction, storage of controlled test materials Access and utilization of automated data for testing programs Counseling methods to advise on various testing programs
1702	General Education and Training	Training Design and Development	Foreign language learning Instructional methods Statistical analysis Research / evaluation Review human research protocols Develop innovations in instructional methods Learning theory, psychology of learning Instructional design practices Educational evaluation Instructional product development Human research protection procedures Statistical analysis Improve instructional practices
2210	Information Technology Management	Customer Support	Apply systems integration methods Project management principles and methods Coordinate installation of new products or equipment Apply operating systems software principles Troubleshoot procedures Configure end user systems components Apply customer support concepts Troubleshoot and recover systems and files Coordination of installation, upgrade and maintenance Communications systems management products Third party software, security packages Scheduling systems and software packages

★ *The HR Specialist will be looking for these keywords in your federal resume. Some of these words would be used for HEADLINES FOR THE OUTLINE FORMAT.*

STAR06

Pay attention!

The entire USAJOBS application process—from the original profile to the actual application in the "Application Manager"—may involve checking as many as 10 boxes about your status as a military spouse. If you intend to use the hiring authorities available to military spouses, you must be very careful to make sure that you check off all the required boxes. Yes, you'll be asked some of the same questions—and it will feel redundant —but please be thorough! Read each of the profile personnel questions and carefully answer the questions. It's important that the human resources specialists can see that you are a military spouse of an active duty member of the Armed Forces, so that you can use this hiring authority.

12. PPP Registered Mil Spouse - Are you a Military Spouse of an Active Duty Military Member of the U.S. Armed Force (including the U.S. Coast Guard and full-time National Guard) and registered in the DoD Priority Placement Program (PPP) Program S?

- A. Yes
- B. No

Apply for Jobs on USAJOBS: Answer Spouse Questions

PROFILE / PREFERENCE INFO: Answer these questions. Each agency collects its own information on preferences and hiring authorities.

---

6. EO 13473 - Are you the spouse of a member of the Armed Forces who has been issued orders for a permanent change of station (PCS)? If yes, confirm that you are indicated on the PCS orders; and you
• have been married to the military member on or prior to the date of your spouse's PCS orders
• are relocating with your spouse to the new duty location AND
• have not previously been appointed using this authority under these orders.
-OR-
Are you the spouse of a member of the Armed Forces who retired with a disability rating at the time of retirement of 100 percent or the spouse of a member of the Armed Forces who retired or separated from the Armed Forces and has a disability rating of 100 percent from the Department of Veterans Affairs?
-OR-
Are you the un-remarried widow or widower of a member of the Armed Forces killed while in active duty status?

For more information, review USAJOBS Veterans resources.

⦿ A.   Yes
○ B.   No

EACH AGENCY IS DIFFERENT. Each agency application will ask about Special Appointing Authorities or Military Spouse Hiring Authority in a different way.

---

16   Are you eligible for noncompetitive appointment under a Special Appointing Authority (this includes employees covered by an Interchange Agreement)?

⦿ Yes
○ No

*   16.1   If you are eligible for noncompetitive appointment under a Special Appointing Authority, what authority are you applying under?

EO 13473, Military Spouse

225 characters left (maximum 250)

STAR07

Hot Tip!

Some USAJOBS announcements do NOT list the documents required for military spouse applications. They will almost always list all of the documents needed from certain groups, like Veterans and Schedule A (disabled) applicants. But they might not list the documents required for military spouses.

The bottom line here is that the human resources specialist must see certain documents to qualify you for your hiring authority, E.O. 13473, and for you to be eligible for the position. Yes, that's the case even if the job announcement doesn't ask for those documents specifically.

Read the required documents section for the list of documents. If they don't list documents for E.O. 13473, upload the PCS orders and your marriage certificate. Remember, if you lack PCS orders, that's okay, because under the National Defense Authorization Act of 2019, all military spouses of active duty military members may apply for federal positions. The marriage certificate is still required.

Military Spouse Authority Eligibility Documents

To use the Military Spouse Hiring Authority, you need to prove your eligibility. Make sure you are aware of required and recommended documents.

- ✪ **Required: A copy of your marriage license**

- ✪ **Required: Other relevant documents**, such as your SF-50 or DD-214 if you are either a prior federal employee or service member.

- ✪ **Required: Your federal resume (Builder or Upload format)**
  Although you can use the resume builder to submit your information in USAJOBS, there are advantages to upload your resume as a PDF or Word document so that you can format the resume to be more readable. If you do upload your resume, make sure you have all of the required information included in your resume.

- ✪ **Required: PCS Orders**
  The PCS orders are really required. Upload your service member's active duty order. Your name does not have to be on the document, but you do need to be authorized as a dependent on the orders.

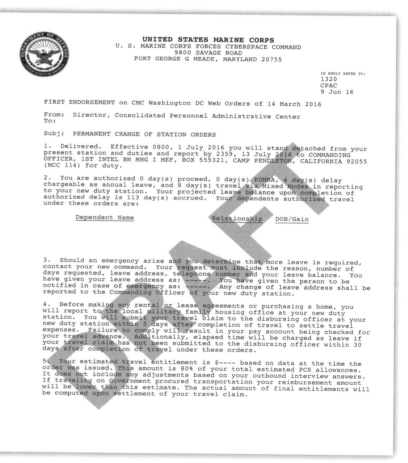

Beware!

Required Documents —

The following required document details have been sourced from the job posting.

The following documents are required if you are applying to this announcement:

The following documents are required and must be provided with your application. Other documents may be required based on the eligibility/eligibilities you are claiming. Click here to view the AF Civilian Employment Eligibility Guide and the required documents you must submit to substantiate the eligibilities you are claiming.

This USJAOBS announcement did not list any documents for Military Spouses.

JUST KNOW that you must upload Marriage Certificate and PCS Orders. Your name does not have to be on the PCS Orders, but you do need to be authorized as a dependent on the orders.

BOOK 248

Marriage Certificat

State of Nevada |
County of Clark, } ss.

No. A 175632

This is to Certify that the undersigned   JUSTICE DAVID ZE

did on the _____   day of _____   A. D. 19

Wedlock   ELVIS ARON PRESLEY

of   MEMPHIS   State of TENNES

Not up-to-date

Some of the instructions in the actual applications are not up-to-date for military spouses.

- They might state that you must travel with your spouse on PCS Orders to use E.O. 13473. This is not true anymore. ANY spouse of Active Duty Military can apply to "military spouse" announcements with E.O. 13473.

- They might state that you MUST be registered in PPP to utilize E.O. 13473. This is not true. In fact, some installations are not registering spouses in PPP any longer. The PPP system is changing.

PART 02

Military Spouse Case Studies

Six military spouses offered to share their federal job search stories and resumes for this book. Each of these incredible spouses is proud of their support for the military's mission, their spouse's service, their families, and America. We're also proud of them and thankful for their willingness to share their stories.

How Did We Meet the Real Military Spouses in These Case Studies?

Kathryn shares these true stories about the women in our case studies:

Nicole | Page 46: Nicole came to one of our "Stars Are Lined Up for Military Spouses" classes. She learned that, in addition to adding her volunteer experience and prior corporate work in her resume, she could also feature her cookie entrepreneurial business. See her cookies and a full introduction on page 15.

Bobbi | Page 58: Bobbi has been working at the Resume Place and is also a military spouse. Kathryn accompanied Bobbi to her PPP interview with HRO at Ft. Meade, MD. It was a memorable three-hour meeting and was one of the inspiring moments that created the first edition of this book. These PPP meetings are going away now. Since we first met, Bobbi's resume has evolved and improved. When she is looking to go federal again, she'll be ready to go.

Jan | Page 69: I met Jan at one of our "Stars Are Lined Up for Military Spouses" classes. She had been a military spouse for years, an Army Community Service (ACS) Director, and was also Ten Steps Certified. Her resume, though, wasn't where it needed to be and was still in Big Block format. I coached her on developing accomplishments and incorporating them into the resume. When she moved to the Washington, DC, area, she landed a fantastic GS-14 position.

Ann | Page 79: I met Ann while teaching a Ten Steps Certification class in Honolulu. Ann was being coached by one of the re-certifying class members, who told me that Ann hadn't been able to work in 22 years as a military spouse. I just *had* to meet her! So I did, and I learned her story, and helped her with her first federal resume. Guess what: she was hired into a government job with that first resume.

Natalie | Page 86: I ran a contest asking military spouses to write about their PCS history and their skills as a spouse. I knew it wouldn't be a popular contest; after all, most don't know how to write about their PCS history and their "career" as a military spouse. Natalie was the ONLY person who wrote to me with her story as part of the contest. But that bravery translated into something exciting for her (and us)! With her first federal resume, she will be hired for her first full-time federal job at her next installation.

Jennifer | Page 96: I met Jennifer after she wrote to me with her story. She told me how her partner would be out of the military in a few years and she wanted to land a great job so that her family could be on the right footing after leaving military service. Armed with her new federal resume that highlighted her military spouse status, she landed an administrative position at the GS-9 level and is working to finish her MBA.

 After you look at these cases, then it will be your turn!
Get started on YOUR federal resume with our effective writing activities in Part 4 starting on page 118.

CASESTUDY

NICOLE BLACK

Jobseeker Facts:

Authorized for E.O. 13473

Entrepreneur

Volunteer

Business experience

Photo: Nicole is an entrepreneur and talented baker. Her company, Cookie Rookie, created these gems for the Resume Place.

Federal Career Objectives:

- ✪ Administrative Specialist, GS-0301-07
- ✪ Inventory Management Specialist, GS-2010-07
- ✪ Contact Representative, GS-0962-07

Successful Federal Job Results:

- ✪ Nicole is PCSing again next year and just beginning her federal job search.
- ✪ *Federal Job Search Activities:* Nicole attended a Stars Are Lined Up class at Army Community Services at Ft. Rucker, AL, during a military spouse appreciation event and received help with her federal resume!

Key Questions:

"I haven't worked for 11 years, so how can I write a federal resume?"

"Should I add my Cookie Rookie company to my resume?"

CORRECT Military Spouse Federal Resume
4 Pages; Outline Format with Accomplishments

NICOLE BLACK

Fort Rucker, AL 36362

(785) 555-5555 • nicoleblack77@gmail.com

MILITARY SPOUSE PREFERENCE: Spouse of Active Duty U.S. Army soldier. Eligible for consideration under Executive Order 13473, September 11, 2009, Non-competitive Appointment for Certain Military Spouses.

> ★ E.O. 13473 right up front!

U.S. ARMY MILITARY SPOUSE PCS ORDER HISTORY:
- Fort Rucker, AL, U.S. Army Aviation, Mar 2018 to present
- Fort Drum, NY, 10th Mountain Division AVN, Mar 2015 to Mar 2018
- Fort Rucker, AL, U.S. Army Aviation, Jun 2012 to Mar 2015
- Fort Riley, 1st Infantry Division AVN, Feb 2007 to Jun 2012

> ★ PCS History added to the Summary at the top

SUMMARY OF SKILLS: U.S. Army Military spouse with 10+ years' experience delivering thorough and skillful administrative support to senior executives and sales teams. Adept at producing proposals, reports and letters, routing incoming mail, managing schedules, and updating and tracking documents. Effective in delivering product consultation and training. Working knowledge of PC/Mac Microsoft® Office (Word, Excel, Power Point, Outlook, Access) and Adobe software applications (Reader, Photoshop).

> ★ Summary of Skills mentions U.S. Army Military Spouse!

EDUCATION

BACHELOR OF ARTS (B.A.)

Adams State University • Alamosa, CO
- — Major: Exercise Physiology & Leisure Sciences / K-12 Education
- — Minor: Business

PROFESSIONAL EXPERIENCE

OWNER   **03/2013 – Present**

Cookie Rookie • Fort Rucker, AL   20 hours per week

Supervisor: Self

Manage all operations of a home-based custom cookie decorating business, including sales, customer service, cookie design/decoration, social media communications, and billing.

> ★ The entrepreneurial cookie business IS relevant for federal positions

CORRESPONDENCE MANAGEMENT AND CUSTOMER SERVICE: Respond to customer inquiries through text, email, or social media accounts (Instagram, Facebook, Pinterest, Messenger) to confirm quotes and pertinent order details. Manage all customer orders by verifying budget, designs, flavors, colors, and quantities. Track customer order due dates each week to ensure accuracy and avoid scheduling conflicts. Contact customers to respond to inquiries, provide order updates, or notify customer of design changes.

> ★ Outline Format with Keywords

RESEARCH, ANALYSIS, AND PLANNING: Research and sketch out unique and creative designs by determining all background, color, overlay, and design options to render cohesive themes for customers. Stage and photograph all completed cookies. Research new products and techniques to incorporate into designs.

1

INVENTORY CONTROL AND PROPERTY ACCOUNTABILITY: Determine best design options and meticulously organize stencils, molds, and tools required to complete orders. Evaluate supply levels monthly and purchase all low stock items and special request materials (cutters, stencils, molds) through online sources.

BUDGET PLANNING AND FINANCIAL MANAGEMENT: Calculate costs of supplies and other expenses based on estimates and price lists. Track incoming revenue through PayPal and ensure expenditures are timed and within budget constraints. Confer with customers to determine appropriate theme schematics, budget, design layouts, and general order basics. Estimate order requirements and costs. Generate customer invoices and track payment daily via Excel.

COMPUTER AND SOFTWARE EXPERTISE: Utilize PicMonkey and Fotor for editing and watermarking photos and Microsoft® Word for design templates. Upload digital cookie photos to various social business accounts for marketing exposure.

KEY ACCOMPLISHMENTS:

— Met corporate request by Resume Place to reproduce all of the company, book, and website logos for publication of an article and book on helping military spouses write Federal resumes. The logos were unique and intricate, and I met a tight deadline.

— Successfully delivered up to 300 cookies for school events, with 5 designs and logos and up to 5 colors total. Customers were very satisfied.

Accomplishments added to stand out!

ADMINISTRATIVE COORINATOR (VOLUNTEER)   09/2017 – 03/2018
Parent Teacher Organization (PTO)   5 Hours per Week
West Carthage Elementary • Carthage, NY
Supervisor: Natalie Jones, 311-411-5111, May Contact

Provided comprehensive, school-wide administrative and clerical support to the teachers and staff at an elementary school with over 400 students located near Fort Drum.

WORK PLANNING AND SCHEDULING: Assembled and packaged all program materials for students and disseminated to each class. Organized and compiled all completed classroom materials and labeled by teacher for dissemination. Ensured all shifts were covered for PTO events by cross-referencing volunteer lists.

FILE MANAGEMENT: Assisted library staff in sorting, clipping, and tracking all box top submissions. Organized and labeled library books in preparation of a new coding system.

KEY ACCOMPLISHMENTS:

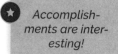

Accomplishments are interesting!

— Contributed 100+ hours of service at various PTO events/fundraisers throughout the year, which helped the school to generate $10K.

— Spearheaded the "Helping Hands" program by providing teachers and staff weekly ongoing assistance with classroom projects, including cutting, assembling, laminating, events planning, and supervising students.

LEAD SALES COORDINATOR

10/2007 – 05/2009

CivicPlus • 1012 Main St., Manhattan, KS 33434
Supervisor: Francis Belacourt, 611-511-4111, May Contact

40 Hours per Week

Provided high-level administrative support for an Inc. 5000 web development company with 2,500+ local government clients nationwide. Supported four-member nationwide executive sales team. Coordinated sales support functions and customer relations.

CORRESPONDENCE MANAGEMENT: Prepared and typed final administration forms and related documents. Uploaded all new correspondence to folder on company server. Conceptualized, implemented, and conducted training on company background, procedures, forms, and FAQs for all new sales executives. Composed proposal responses and email correspondence for new clients.

REPORT PRODUCTION: Used office automation software packages and equipment to type, edit, and format letters, email responses, and responses to Request for Proposals (RFP). Reformatted templates, composed case studies of new clients, and added pictures within text to explain procedural steps. Created, maintained, and analyzed all sales forecasting/revenue spreadsheets for sales team in Microsoft® Excel. Provided monthly spreadsheets/graphs to CEO and VP Sales to make company projections and track sales.

Outline Format with Keywords

CONTRACT REVIEW AND ANALYSIS: Identified all qualified prospective bids, determined whether requirements were feasible, and outlined response structure. Independently wrote and tailored each highly technical proposal response for appropriate government agencies and associations requesting web design/consulting services. Evaluated and printed all sales materials and proposal items weekly for team.

KEY ACCOMPLISHMENTS:

— Promoted to Lead Coordinator in 2008 and proactively revamped the Coordinator role to ensure proper coverage of all bids. Once Coordinators were aligned and sales processes better streamlined to handle more complex bids, I implemented ongoing training on department policies and procedures for all incoming coordinators and sales executives, thus ensuring consistency of sales processes and bid guidelines.

— By conducting frequent team training and weekly discussions, as well as initiating weekly calls with assigned Sales Executives, I led my team to produce 60+ RFPs each month (up from 20), helping take the company from $2.8M to $4.5M/year.

ORDER ANALYST

03/2006 – 07/2007

Oracle (formerly NextAction) • 111 West Street, Westminster, CO
Supervisor: Maximillian DeLaCeur, 811-922-8222, Contact Me First

40 Hours per Week

Created, organized, and managed documents and reports in a CRM system. Worked with clients' technical staff to ensure data files were transferred and downloaded for specific product model builds. Provided model reports to key clients. Assisted sales with up-selling.

DOCUMENT MANAGEMENT: Filed and retrieved company documents and reports. Created new folders on server housing all client reports, orders, and routine requests as needed. Worked with clients' technical staff to ensure necessary data files were transferred, downloaded, and used appropriately for product model builds. Provided overall model reports to key clients and assisted Sales with up-sell possibilities through reports.

KEY ACCOMPLISHMENT:

— Developed profitable relationships with clients based on excellent customer service and thorough understanding of a client's needs for a more targeted email campaign approach. Utilized internal resources across model building to ensure a 100% accurate and on-time statistical model.

SALES SUPPORT REPRESENTATIVE
Experian • Costa Mesa, CA
Supervisor: Jessica Jamison, jamisonj@ex.p.an.com, Contact Me First

01/2001 – 02/2006
40 Hours per Week

TRAVEL MANAGEMENT: Researched rates for airfare, hotel, and car rental for all domestic travel. Created, submitted, and tracked travel arrangements and travel expense reimbursement for solo trips.

KEY ACCOMPLISHMENTS:

— Main point of contact for all credit, collections, and fraud departments for the three Top Tier banks in my area. Proactively contacted each group monthly to track concerns or training needs. Increased sales by 8% each year for each account.

— Performed sales support duties for a team of three sales representatives for a catalog marketing company that housed data on 65M+ consumers. I improved and streamlined the sales leads process by establishing an Excel-based tracking system.

CUSTOMER SERVICE MANAGER
Shortland Publications (McGraw-Hill) • Columbus, OH   40 Hours per Week
Supervisor: Sheryl Knickerbocker, 711-611-5111, May Contact

02/1998 – 12/2000

PROPERTY ACCOUNTABILITY: Checked inventory records to determine availability of requested merchandise before processing purchase orders. Immediately notified client by phone of any anticipated shipping delays or concerns. Alerted fulfillment staff of all large future orders to ensure inventory was available.

KEY ACCOMPLISHMENT:

— Managed more than 1,000 accounts and supported 20 sales representatives in their selling efforts. Processed all outbound and inbound orders, totaling $3M+ in revenue per year. Tracked product and inventory counts weekly through company portal and provided written updates.

BEFORE Federal Resume
3 Pages: Not Targeted, No Cookie Business

Nicole Black
Fort Rucker, AL 36362
(785) 555-5555 | nicoleblack77@gmail.com

SPOUSE PREFERENCE: Spouse of Active Duty US Army soldier. Eligible for consideration under Executive Order 13473, September 11, 2009 Non-competitive Appointment for Certain Military Spouses.

SUMMARY OF SKILLS: Over ten years' experience providing thorough and skillful administrative support to senior executives and sales teams. Specialized in process flow and acting as intermediary between corporate-level officers and clients, while ensuring deadlines are consistently met. Consistently delivered exemplary customer service, and attention to detail organization in a fast paced, high stress environment.

VOLUNTEER EXPERIENCE

PTA VOLUNTEER   03/2018 - 05/2018
Fort Rucker Primary School, Fort Rucker, AL   3 Hours per Week
Supervisor: Jeorge Jennings, jjennings@frps.edu   Okay to contact this Supervisor: Yes

GENERAL WORK: Worked as a part of the Parent Teacher Association (PTA) team. Prepared and packaged over 800 bags of popcorn for all students for end of year celebration. Requested specifically by teacher to tie-dye shirts for Kindergarten pods for multiple end of year events. Provided assistance and guidance to students during Field Day activities, ensuring they followed set safety rules. Presented student artwork throughout school.

PTO VOLUNTEER   09/2017 - 03/2018
West Carthage Elementary, Carthage, NY   5 Hours per Week
Supervisor: Natalie Jones, 311-411-5111   Okay to contact this Supervisor: Yes

GENERAL CLERICAL: Spearheaded the "Helping Hands" program by providing teachers and staff ongoing assistance with various in and out of classroom projects. Assembled and packaged all program materials for students, then disseminated to each class. Assisted parents and students at Scholastic Book Fair by helping complete order forms, processing orders, and securing items each night. Prepared, packaged, and sold 100+ bags of popcorn to students, teachers, and staff each week. Ensured all popcorn funds were counted and till was 100% balanced. Monitored popcorn inventory levels and alerted PTO of any deficiencies. Prepared many books in library by relabeling current stickers in anticipation of a new coding system. Cut, assembled, and tracked box tops. Opened and organized incoming boxed shipments, and placed items in numerical order for easy pickup. Consistently took on shifts where volunteers were lacking.

Key Accomplishment:
+ Contributed 100+ hours of service at various PTO events/fundraisers throughout the year, which has helped the school to generate funds totaling over $10k+ for the school year. Monies generated from all fundraisers help support many staff functions, school appreciation events, and provide new equipment/supplies for teachers, staff, and students throughout the year.

PROFESSIONAL EXPERIENCE

LEAD SALES COORDINATOR   10/2007 - 05/2009
CivicPlus, Manhattan, KS   40 Hours per Week
Salary: 42,000.00 Per Year   **Supervisor:** Francis Belacourt, 611-511-4111   Okay to contact this Supervisor: Yes

ROUTINE REQUEST RESPONSES: Prepared and typed in final form administration forms and related documents. Uploaded all new correspondence to folder on company server. Conceptualized and implemented training, conducting training on company background, procedures, forms, and FAQ's for all new sales executives. Maintained calendar and scheduled appointments for nationwide Sales Executive team with authority to commit Executive's time based on knowledge of his/her interests, commitments, and work schedule

PREPARE AND REVIEW CORRESPONDENCE: Identified qualified prospective bids, determined whether requirements are feasible, then outlined response structure. Independently wrote and catered each highly technical

The Cookie Rookie business is missing. Not good! She needs this experience on the resume.

This BEFORE resume is in the Outline Format (good). She worked with Mike Kozlowski on this federal resume! We improved her resume with the Cookie Rookie business and her PCS History.

proposal response for viable government agencies and associations requesting web design/consulting services. Evaluated, modified, and printed all sales materials and proposal items weekly for team.

OFFICE AUTOMATION: Used office automation software packages and equipment to produce letters, emails, and Request for Proposals. Created, maintained, and analyzed all sales forecasting/revenue spreadsheets for Sales team through Excel. Provided monthly spreadsheets/graphs to CEO and VP Sales to make company projections and track Sales goals. All items are completed with no supervision. Created and gathered all forms, procedures, letters, proposal templates, forecast/revenue spreadsheets, graphs, meeting agenda/minutes, and marketing collateral into folders and placed onto company portal. Ensured accurate updates on all folder items each month. Organized and maintained all contract paperwork.

ADMINISTRATION AND MANAGEMENT: Identified leads through various online and government sites/publications, referrals, and GSA postings before distributing to sales team. Liaised between Sales and company department heads to create a more streamlined process for new clients among the various teams. Managed and coordinated weekly tasks for 4 employees, allowing for mentoring opportunities and avoid task crossover. Attended monthly company meetings, provided department updates and sales projections. Recorded minutes, typed, and emailed to Sales team upon request. Ordered recurring items, organized and dispensed materials to recipients.

COMPUTER SKILLS: Utilized Microsoft Suite programs for creating forecasting reports/graphs, team procedure documents and forms, and generating proposal templates/responses and presentation materials. Typing speed is 50 wpm. Typed documents from rough draft into final form, ensuring accuracy with regard to format, spelling, grammar, punctuation, and distribution of copies.

Key Accomplishments:

+ Provided high level administrative functions to an INC.5000 company that serves over 2,500+ local government clients nationwide, consisting of over 55K government users. At the time of hiring, I was the only Sales Coordinator supporting 4 Sales Executives. My primary function was to research and qualify all leads, then create and submit 20+ Request For Proposals a month.

+ With the company expanding so quickly, 3 Coordinators and 6 additional Sales Executives were hired to try and launch a global sales approach. I was promoted as Lead in 2008 and proactively revamped the Coordinator role to ensure proper coverage of all bids by Coordinator and their respective Sales Executives' territories. Once Coordinators were aligned and sales processes better streamlined to handle more complex bids, I implemented ongoing trainings for all incoming Coordinators and Sales Executives on department policies and procedures, ensuring consistency of all sales processes and bid guidelines.

+ By conducting frequent team training and weekly discussions, while also initiating weekly calls with assigned Sales Executives, I was able to help my team produce 60+ RFP's a month in a more consistent and accurately detailed manner, helping take the company from $2.8M to $4.5M/year. The company has consistently grown by 25% year over year since 2008.

ORDER ANALYST   **03/2006 - 07/2007**
Oracle (formerly NextAction), Westminster, CO   40 Hours per Week
Salary: 40,000.00 Per Year   **Supervisor**: Maximillian DeLaCeur, 811-922-8222   Contact me first

ORGANIZE AND MAINTAIN INFORMATION: File and retrieve company documents and reports. Created new folders on server that houses all client reports, orders, and all routine request items as needed. Maintains records on correspondence and action items to ensure timely reply or action. Worked with clients' technical staff to ensure necessary data files transferred, downloaded, and used appropriately for particular product model builds. Provided overall model reports to key clients and assisted Sales with any up-sell possibilities through the use of these reports.

TRACKING AND FOLLOW-UP: Tracked progression of the catalog list product models to insure timely completion of list order, to meet client (Cataloger) deadlines. Communicated often with new clients to ensure order accuracy and provide ongoing status updates. Proactively reviewed fulfillment lists once complete ensuring household counts were accurate and models were run correctly.

MAINTAIN WORKING RELATIONSHIPS: Synchronized order project coordination between technical account managers and production analysts for models built based on statistical techniques. Cooperatively work with client and all company departments to ensure order accuracy and timely completion. Acted as liaison between client and analytical teams when orders were inaccurate; expressed tact and professionalism to resolve any disagreements.

Key Accomplishments:

+ Developed profitable relationships with clients based on excellent customer service, plus thorough understanding and assessing of client's needs for a more targeted email campaign approach. Consistently following up with clients and utilizing internal resources throughout the entire stages of model building ultimately ensured a 100% accurate and early/on-time statistical model.

SALES SUPPORT REPRESENTATIVE   01/2001 - 02/2006

Experian, Costa Mesa, CA   40 Hours per Week

Salary: 35,000.00 Per Year   **Supervisor**: Jessica Jamison, jamisonj@ex.p.an.com   Contact me first

ADMINISTRATION AND CLERICAL: Researched, created, submitted, and tracked travel arrangements and travel expense reimbursement for solo trips. Managed day-to-day sales operations in establishing new clients into cooperative prospect database, by entering all pertinent client data/status updates into company portal and Access database. Qualified prospects through various online sources, catalog database publications, referrals, and incoming Sales calls. Organized and calendared business lunch/dinner meetings with clientele for self or Sales Executives as necessary.

SENIOR LEADER SUPPORT: Worked closely in conjunction with Senior Management, Sales, Account Management, Analytics and Production to accomplish revenue goals. Provided marketing materials, sales updates, and onboarding instructions to prospective/new clients from trade shows. Consistently coordinated efforts within the company to get clients signed onto new products and services. Supported a team of Account Executives by taking the lead on various potential sales opportunities to meet and exceed client revenue goals. Provided ongoing Credit, Fraud, and Collections trainings to Associates, Managers, and Department heads within all lines of business (Card, Home Finance, Auto Finance, Student Lending) for Chase Bank, Wells Fargo, and Bank of America.

ORAL COMMUNICATION: Grew and managed banking relationships by consistently evaluating all business needs for Chase Bank, Bank of America, and Wells Fargo clients. Provided excellent daily support and consistent process improvement strategies over phone, on-site visit, or email. Proactively made prospect calls to various contacts within a Strategic Banking Institution as part of a major data cleansing initiative. Managed and resolved client concerns, coordinated with internal resources to ensure client satisfaction.

Key Accomplishments:

+ Main point of contact for all credit, collections, and fraud departments within each of the 3 Top Tier banks in my area, and I proactively contacted each group monthly to track any concerns or training needs. Having made frequent contact and providing ongoing training services helped the company establish more of a foothold, which ultimately increased sales by 8% each year for each of my accounts.

+ Performed sales support duties for a team of 3 sales representatives for a catalog marketing company that housed data on over 65M consumers. In the 3 years I worked for the company, I was able to help improve the sales leads process by establishing a new tracking system in Excel that made it easier to distribute leads more fairly to each rep and provide sales forecasts to President of company each month. All leads and newly on-boarded clients now had to be tracked through me. This efficiency helped streamline the entire sales lead process and stop the sales reps from stealing leads from one another. This helped increase efficiency by 10%.

EDUCATION

BACHELOR OF ARTS (B.A) - 1998
Adams State University
Major: Exercise Physiology and Leisure Sciences/ K-12 Education
Minor: Business GPA: 3.20 of a maximum 4.0

Private Sector Resume
2 Pages: Bullet-style with Boldface Accomplishments

NICOLE BLACK

Fort Rucker, AL 36362 | 785.555.5555 | nicoleblack77@gmail.com

SALES ASSISTANT | ADMINISTRATIVE COORDINATOR
Customer Service ► Executive Team Support ► Sales Coordination

U.S. Army Military Spouse and administrative professional with 10+ years of experience providing sales, customer service, operational, and analytical support to senior executives and sales teams. Skilled in managing schedules, sales orders, and customer relations in fast-paced, deadline-driven environments. Adept at producing proposals, reports, sales analytics, and collateral materials. Strong time management, organization, and communications skills. Culinary entrepreneur with business management experience. Typing speed 50 WPM. B.A. degree.

Expertise Summary: Sales Order Tracking/Management; Database Management; Executive Support; Correspondence/Social Media Management; Customer Service / Customer Relations; AP/AR.
Computer Skills: Microsoft® Office (Word, Excel, PowerPoint, Outlook, Access), PicMonkey, Fotor, and Adobe Photoshop.

Include military spouse mention here—optional!

Summary of skills must match the target advertisement

PROFESSIONAL EXPERIENCE

BUSINESS OWNER / MANAGER
Cookie Rookie, Fort Rucker, AL

3/2013 – Present

Manage all operations of a home-based custom cookie decorating business, including sales, customer service, cookie design/decoration, social media communications, and billing. Develop artwork proposals and create customized designs to meet customer budgets. Manage sales lifecycle through order delivery.

- Conceptualize and manage all facets of business startup.
- Bake, design, decorate, package and ship customized cookie designs to customers throughout the U.S. Photograph, edit, watermark, and post selected cookie photos to social media/business accounts.
- Created Excel spreadsheet to improve order tracking and management.
- Leverage food service industry knowledge to maintain the highest levels of cleanliness and quality.

ADMINISTRATIVE COORDINATOR (Volunteer)
Parent Teacher Organization (PTO), West Carthage Elementary School, Carthage, NY

9/2017 – 3/2018

Provided comprehensive, school-wide administrative and clerical support to the teachers and staff at an elementary school with over 400 students located near Fort Drum.

- Spearheaded "Helping Hands" program to provide ongoing, consistent support to teachers and staff with internal and external classroom projects. Coordinated volunteer teams.
- Completed order forms and ensured accurate orders for the annual Scholastic Book Fair.
- Managed weekly popcorn sales to students, teachers, and staff. Managed accounting of funds from popcorn sales and ensured receipts were 100% balanced.
- Contributed over 100+ hours of service for PTO fundraisers annually, which generated $10K+ to support a variety of school events, staff functions, and purchase of new equipment/supplies.

LEAD SALES COORDINATOR
10/2007 – 5/2009
CivicPlus, Manhattan, KS

Provided high-level administrative support for an Inc. 5000 web development company with 2,500+ local government clients nationwide. Supported four-member nationwide executive sales team. Coordinated sales support functions and customer relations.

Keep the accomplish-ments!

▶ **Increased production of Request for Proposals (RFPs) to 60+ monthly from 20; which helped the company to increase sales from $2.8M to $4.5M in sales/year**.

- **Generated Leads:** Used a range of sources to research, identify, and qualify prospective customers for the sales team.

▶ **Streamlined processes for new clients, improving retention.**

Bold type will be the KEYWORDS!

- **Wrote customized bids and proposals** to target government agencies and associations requesting web design/consulting services.
- **Prepared analytics, forecasts, trends analyses, and reports**: Analyzed sales statistics and prepared forecasts and revenue spreadsheets and graphs for the sales team, CEO, and VP of Sales.
- **Executive Team Schedule Management**: Maintained calendars and scheduled appointments for a nationwide Sales Executive Team.
- **Created Client Communications**: Wrote, edited, and prepared final sales proposals and collateral materials for the sales team. Developed client presentations, correspondence, and emails.

ORDER ANALYST
3/2006 – 7/2007
Oracle (formerly NextAction), Westminster, CO

Created, organized, and managed documents and reports in a CRM system. Worked with clients' technical staff to ensure data files were transferred and downloaded for specific product model builds. Provided model reports to key clients. Assisted sales with up-selling.

- Played key role in assessing a client's needs and developing a more targeted email campaign approach.
- Developed profitable relationships with clients through customer service excellence.
- Consistently followed up with clients and utilized internal resources throughout the entire stages of the model build, which ultimately ensured a 100% accurate and early/on-time statistical model.

ADDITIONAL VOLUNTEER EXPERIENCE

PTA Volunteer, Fort Rucker Primary School, Fort Rucker, AL; 3/2018 – Present

EDUCATION

Bachelor of Arts (B.A.)
Exercise Physiology/Leisure Sciences/K-12 Education; Business Minor
Adams State University, Alamosa, CO

Cover Letter
Target your cover letter to the announcement with keywords

Targeting this position:

Supply Technician, GS-2005-07 US Army Corps of Engineers, Kansas City, Missouri

Target qualifications:

One year of specialized experience which includes experience with property handling, researching data and reports and fact-finding, and/or ensuring supply support for production. This definition of specialized experience is typical of work performed at the next lower grade/level position in the federal service (GS-06).

You will be evaluated on the basis of your level of competency in the following areas:

- ✪ **Inventory Management**
- ✪ **Supply Planning**
- ✪ **Technical Competence**

Responsibilities:

- ✪ Provide a variety of **technical supply support** to a district or laboratory as a member of a USACE Logistics Delivery Point team.

- ✪ Provide assistance for all areas of **supply management** as required to all customer elements, which may include a USACE division headquarters.

- ✪ **Management of expendable/non-expendable items and materials**, which are handled through central supply channels, coordinating direct purchase, and formal procurement procedures that sometimes require extensive fact finding, analysis and research.

- ✪ **Conducts physical inventories** of a broad range of diverse, specialized items, some of which are difficult to identify and/or differentiate from others, and which require special treatment in handling and storage.

- ✪ **Prepares recurring and special reports** and compiles statistics from data requiring substantial analysis, interpretation, and development of new formats.

NICOLE BLACK

Fort Rucker, AL 36362 | 785.555.5555 | nicoleblack77@gmail.com

Human Resources Recruiter
US Navy EIC
San Diego, CA
February 14, 2019

Re: Supply Technician, GS-2005-7, Kansas City, MO

To whom it may concern:

I will be relocating to Kansas City, Missouri, where my Active Duty spouse will be stationed for his retirement location. He will not retire until January of 2020. I would like to take this opportunity to be considered for Supply Technician with the Military Spouse Preference until that date.

My relevant experience for the position includes:

- **Inventory Management –** Business Manager, Cookie Rookie, Ft. Rucker, AL. I have managed a successful niche custom cookie production firm for the last 6 years. My inventory includes icing and cutting equipment, specialty molds, production facilities.
- **Supply Planning –** My supply planning is Just-in-Time with orders for military base volunteer groups, corporations, and family events. Supplies are ordered online from vendors and local businesses. My products involve both expendable and non-expendable items purchased through various systems.
- **Technical Competence –** I successfully meet deadlines and ensure customer satisfaction. I utilize software, social media, graphics software, and database systems to mange client and order information

I believe I would be an asset to your organization because I have:

- 6 years' experience in supply and inventory services
- Skills in researching designs, equipment, materials, and negotiating prices from vendors
- Inventory maintained with safety, sanitation, and availability for quick turn orders
- Efficient computer skills for billings, reports, and tax preparation

Finally, as an Active Duty Military Spouse, I have developed solid skills in logistics, problem-solving, planning, and working under deadlines. I would like to offer my skills to USACE. I would be a valuable member of your supply team!

I can interview by Skype or telephone. I will be in Kansas City on September 1. Thank you for your consideration.

Sincerely,

Nicole Black

Attachments: PCS Orders, Marriage Certificate

CASESTUDY

BOBBI ROBBINS

Jobseeker Profile Points:

Activated Reservist Military Spouse, Recent Graduate, Solid Work History, Used E.O. 13473

Photo: Bobbi Robbins holding the Bye-Bye PPP-S cake, standing between Ten Steps to a Federal Job instructors, John Gagnon and Kathryn Troutman, at the Military District of Washington training, JB Anacostia-Bolling, Washington, DC.

Bobbi's Objectives:

- ✪ Administrative Specialist, GS-0301
- ✪ Health Administrative Specialist, GS-0671
- ✪ Program Analyst, GS-0343
- ✪ Training & Education Coordinator, GS-0172

Bobbi's Results:

- ✪ Referred for positions using E.O. 13473 but had to PCS
- ✪ Bobbi now works with Kathryn on the *Stars Are Lined Up for Military Spouses* campaign!

Case Study Exercise

Three versions of Bobbi's resumes are provided: her original 2-page "federal" resume, her corrected federal resume that got her referred multiple times, and her updated private industry resume. **Compare and contrast the following points across the different versions:**

- ✪ Military spouse identification (E.O. 13473)
- ✪ Military spouse mention in professional summary
- ✪ Military spouse experiences as job block content
- ✪ Job block in Outline Format with targeted keywords
- ✪ Accomplishments included

CORRECT Military Spouse Federal Resume
4 Pages: Outline Format with ALL CAP KEYWORDS and Accomplishments

BOBBI ROBBINS
Baltimore, MD 21228 • 443-444-4444 • email@gmail.com
Military Spouse – Authorized for EO 13473, Military Spouse Hiring Authority

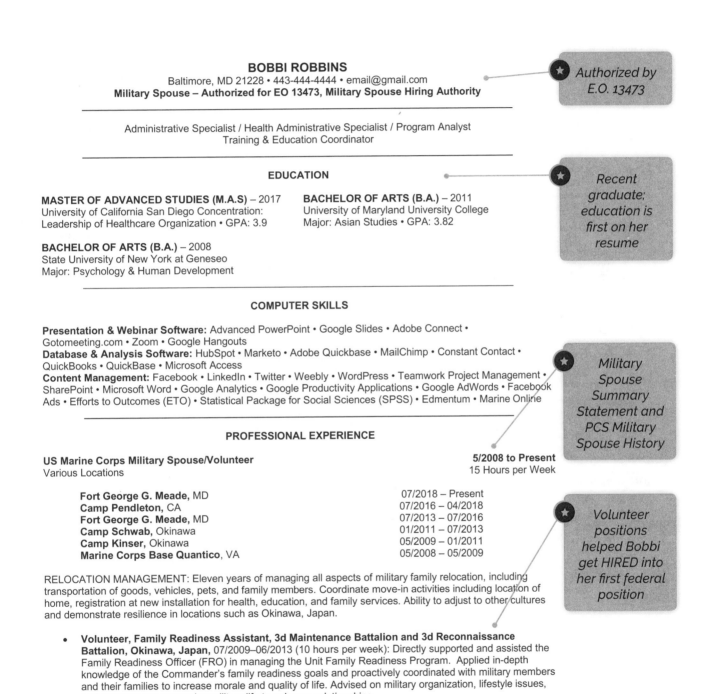

Authorized by E.O. 13473

Administrative Specialist / Health Administrative Specialist / Program Analyst
Training & Education Coordinator

EDUCATION

Recent graduate; education is first on her resume

MASTER OF ADVANCED STUDIES (M.A.S) – 2017
University of California San Diego Concentration:
Leadership of Healthcare Organization • GPA: 3.9

BACHELOR OF ARTS (B.A.) – 2011
University of Maryland University College
Major: Asian Studies • GPA: 3.82

BACHELOR OF ARTS (B.A.) – 2008
State University of New York at Geneseo
Major: Psychology & Human Development

COMPUTER SKILLS

Presentation & Webinar Software: Advanced PowerPoint • Google Slides • Adobe Connect • Gotomeeting.com • Zoom • Google Hangouts
Database & Analysis Software: HubSpot • Marketo • Adobe Quickbase • MailChimp • Constant Contact • QuickBooks • QuickBase • Microsoft Access
Content Management: Facebook • LinkedIn • Twitter • Weebly • WordPress • Teamwork Project Management • SharePoint • Microsoft Word • Google Analytics • Google Productivity Applications • Google AdWords • Facebook Ads • Efforts to Outcomes (ETO) • Statistical Package for Social Sciences (SPSS) • Edmentum • Marine Online

Military Spouse Summary Statement and PCS Military Spouse History

PROFESSIONAL EXPERIENCE

US Marine Corps Military Spouse/Volunteer
Various Locations

5/2008 to Present
15 Hours per Week

Fort George G. Meade, MD	07/2018 – Present
Camp Pendleton, CA	07/2016 – 04/2018
Fort George G. Meade, MD	07/2013 – 07/2016
Camp Schwab, Okinawa	01/2011 – 07/2013
Camp Kinser, Okinawa	05/2009 – 01/2011
Marine Corps Base Quantico, VA	05/2008 – 05/2009

Volunteer positions helped Bobbi get HIRED into her first federal position

RELOCATION MANAGEMENT: Eleven years of managing all aspects of military family relocation, including transportation of goods, vehicles, pets, and family members. Coordinate move-in activities including location of home, registration at new installation for health, education, and family services. Ability to adjust to other cultures and demonstrate resilience in locations such as Okinawa, Japan.

- **Volunteer, Family Readiness Assistant, 3d Maintenance Battalion and 3d Reconnaissance Battalion, Okinawa, Japan,** 07/2009–06/2013 (10 hours per week): Directly supported and assisted the Family Readiness Officer (FRO) in managing the Unit Family Readiness Program. Applied in-depth knowledge of the Commander's family readiness goals and proactively coordinated with military members and their families to increase morale and quality of life. Advised on military organization, lifestyle issues, and stresses accompanying military life to enhance relationships.
- **Volunteer, L.I.N.K.S. Mentor, Marine Corps Community Services, Okinawa, Japan,** 02/2012–06/2013): Worked on a one-on-one and team basis to mentor service members and their families on the

benefits, resources, and services available. Provided mentorship and guidance across Lifestyle, Insights, Networking, Knowledge, and Skills (L.I.N.K.S.). Instructed classes and workshops on a range of topics encompassing the military lifestyle. Delivered information at awareness/briefing sessions and presented key points to specifically targeted audiences, such as parents, children, spouses, etc. Briefed sections of the curriculum at monthly workshops of up to 40 participants.

PROGRAM MANAGER, Ten Steps to a Federal Job Certification   **1/2018 – present**
The Resume Place, Inc., Baltimore, MD   40 Hours per Week
11 Smith Lane, Catonsville, MD 21228   Supervisor: Kathryn Troutman, 443-710-8300, May contact

PROGRAM MANAGER: Manage the activities and requirements of the webinar and in-person training programs associated with the Ten Steps to a Federal Job certification licenses. Provide communication, marketing, and relationship-building services. Identify current trends regarding federal jobs and suggest improvements as applicable.

> ★ *Outline Format with ALL CAP KEYWORDS!*

TRAINING COORDINATION: Plan and update annual training plans. Develop partnerships with military base leadership and employment assistance personnel to draw insights that can translate into training plans with measurable outcomes for Veterans, military spouses, current college students, and recent college graduates.

INSTRUCTOR: Train career coaches and transition assistance professionals on how to help military spouses navigate the Priority Placement Program-Spouses and the benefits of the Military Spouse Program for federal positions through interactive in-person and webinar sessions. Share best practices and provide tips to make the process more approachable for military spouses seeking assistance from these professionals.

Key Accomplishment – Book Contributor and Instructor:
- Contributing Editor and Instructor for the 2nd edition of *The Stars Are Lined Up for Military Spouses*. The book and licensed curriculum are designed to help military spouses understand the special hiring authorities when seeking federal jobs and change their resumes to feature the Military Spouse Volunteer "Job Block" on the Federal and private sector resume.

> ★ *Accomplishments are included!*

PROJECT & PLANNING MANAGER   **10/2017 – 01/2018**
Northern San Diego Health Services   20 Hours per Week
150 Nueva Street, Carlsbad, CA 92055   Supervisor: Bea Carmen, bcarmen@nsdhs.org, Contact me first

PROJECT MANAGEMENT: Provided project leadership for small and mid-sized projects. Built strong cross-functional relationships to ensure that all stakeholders were appropriately engaged. Oversaw timeline, budget, and implementation of project according to approved scope. Implemented processes that supported the strategic and operational business plans. Tracked action items and provided status reports for projects.

CROSS-FUNCTIONAL TEAM MANAGEMENT: Worked cross-functionally with teams to evaluate and assign projects. Promoted smooth workflow and communication between departments. Acted as change management agent to clearly explain the actions needed and return on investment. Participated in strategic project management and problem solving, while appropriately using critical thinking.

PROGRAM PLANNING & GRANTS INTERN   **06/2017 – 09/2017**
Northern San Diego Health Services   20 Hours per Week
150 Nueva Street, Carlsbad, CA 92055   Supervisor: Henry Ortiz, hortiz@nsdhs.org, Contact me first

BUSINESS DEVELOPMENT RESEARCHER: Identified social determinants of health for service areas in the northern section of San Diego county. Aided in the identification of needed services to improve patient outcomes. Recognized trends and notified department leadership. Researched and identified opportunities for business development and partnerships. Identified gaps and new areas for problem solving.

GRADUATE STUDENT   09/2016 – 09/2017
University of California San Diego, San Diego, CA   16 Hours per Week
1100 Green Street, San Diego, CA 92122   Advisor: Robert Kraemer, rkraemer@ucalsd.edu, May contact

PROJECT MANAGEMENT: Assessed internal and external factors to determine competitive situations for organizations. Developed strategic plans and processes to successfully implement changes in healthcare organizations. Applied principles of a project management professional and Lean methodologies to analyze situations, plan designs, and manage improvements to operations.

FINANCIAL MANAGEMENT AND ACCOUNTING: Applied the principles of capital structure and cash management to plan budgets and generate financial reports pertaining to healthcare delivery costs. Develop short- and long-range financial forecasts. Employed benchmarking techniques in business planning.

PROGRAM MANAGER/CAREER COACH   08/2015 – 07/2016
Johns Hopkins Health System, Baltimore, MD   40 Hours per Week
25 Light Street, Baltimore, MD 21287   Supervisor: Yolanda Dennison, ydennison@jh.edu, May contact

PROJECT MANAGER: Worked with nursing staff to identify critical shortages for entry level staff. Worked in the Office of Strategic Workforce Planning and Development (SWPD) to create staff training pipelines to address some of this need. Ensured that position-related skills assessments were still currently relevant for the role. Managed the expectations and engagement of all stakeholders including the departmental leadership of Human Resources and Nursing as well as the entry-level staff and community members aspiring for employment by ensuring that goals and requirements were clear and well-communicated.

STRATEGIC PLANNING: Facilitated SWPD meetings with Nursing department leadership to assess projected staffing needs and identify appropriate tactics to align resources to ensure adequate staffing. Leveraged resources to do create workforce pipelines to address some of the hospital's future staffing needs.

Key Accomplishment:
- Implemented a new program designed to bring qualified graduating high school seniors in to address the need for qualified Clinical Technicians. Lead a team consisting of the Baltimore City Public School Liaison, Johns Hopkins nursing, staff from the Baltimore County Community College, and SWPD staff to establish the training program for these high school graduates. Eight students were accepted into the pilot offering.

Great! More accomplishments!

PROCESS ANALYST: Observed and evaluated existing administrative practices and then established a structured and efficient process for the intake of new Clinical Technicians (nurse extenders) in the Nursing department's SOARING program. Facilitated the smooth onboarding of 75 new hires in 3 cohorts, helping to uphold organization mission and values. Provided the SOARING team with aggregated assessment summaries for each candidate. Created a desktop procedures manual for the role of Career Coach operating at the Johns Hopkins Hospital site, as opposed to being stationed in the administrative suites off-site. This enabled a smooth transition for new coaches with minimal disruption to the more than 800 clients served. Improved the flow of clients by streamlining the intake process.

CAREER NAVIGATOR: Served as a career coach and guide for over 800 entry- to mid-level employees seeking career counseling and skills-upgrading/enhancement. Hosted information sessions to highlight new and critical roles for these employees in support of the organization's "grow our own" philosophy. Arranged and/or administered assessments through a health system career assessment center. Provided follow-up counseling to employees, which enabled them to receive the job training required to earn a promotion or transition to other viable positions within the organization. Performed case management and data management duties to record, monitor, and report participants' progress using Efforts to Outcome (ETO) software.

FAMILY READINESS OFFICER (FRO), (NF-0301-04)   11/2009 – 02/2013
Marine Corps Community Services, Okinawa, Japan   40 Hours per Week
Supervisors: Colonel Jeremy Hall, jeremy.hall@usmc.mil, May contact
            Colonel Stephen Newsome, stephen.newsome@usmc.mil, May contact

CLIENT SUPPORT & NEEDS ASSESSMENTS: Conducted biannual surveys to assess needs of families and personnel to increase the program's value and to inform leadership of targeted suggestions for implementing information and assistance systems for spouses and service members. Provided support and assistance to the Marines, Sailors, and their families through weekly informational email communications and newsletters. Advised all personnel of the merits of the Unit, Personnel, & Family Readiness Program (UPFRP).

POLICIES AND PROCEDURES SUBJECT MATTER EXPERT: Adhered to the Marine Corps Order (MCO) 1754.9 and then MCO 1754.9A orders that governed UPFRP. Provided leadership with a summary of the order and advised them of actions that could be taken within its parameters, especially as they applied to units based in Okinawa. Served as the conduit between family members and the Command, bringing their needs to the attention of leadership and reassuring them that they have support available in the Command.

COMMAND AND COMMUNITY LIAISON: Represented the Commanding Officer at conferences and meetings with high-ranking American and Japanese officials, providing accurate information on the needs of the service members and their families and bringing local and non-governmental contractors to support various unit events.

Key Accomplishment:
- Collaborated with FROs across five 3d Marine Division units and other outside organizations, such as the Camp Courtney Junior Marines, to plan and execute the first-ever annual 3d Marine Division Marine Corps Birthday Ball for Kids. More than 250 children participated in this event that provided an understanding of the ethos behind their parents' service in a way that was relatable. I was presented an award for "superior accomplishment and/or personal effort that contributed to improvement of the quality and efficiency of an MCCS operation." Children's birthday balls continue to be a best practice for Marine Corps units across the country and overseas.

> ★ *Accomplishments will help you get REFERRED and Invited to the Interview!*

WORK & FAMILY LIFE EXPERT: Managed the presence of program resource specialists at major unit events to increase accessibility. Wrote instructional guidance delegating work for 15 volunteers across 3 geographically separated bases who coordinated other volunteer groups to execute morale and training events. Wrote after action reports after major events/trainings to analyze what worked and what needed improvement in future opportunities. Facilitated and taught monthly classes, such as Understanding the Okinawa Area Emergency Evacuation Plan, based on the needs of the command and the community. Connected outbound personnel and family members with FROs at their gaining command.

FINANCIAL MANAGEMENT & ADVICE: Managed annual Unit Family Readiness budgets of up to $17,000. Allocated funds and donated items while ensuring that spending stayed within the guidelines stipulated for Non-Appropriated Funds. Coordinated with active duty personnel to have Appropriated Funds offset some of the cost of unit events, keeping within the authorized budget and spending guidelines.

COMMUNICATION MANAGEMENT: Used MS Excel, MS Outlook, and Marine Online to maintain distribution lists of up to 750 Marines spread throughout up to six companies and their family members. Used distribution lists to facilitate home and section visits as well as telephone, post, and email communications to maximize awareness of the program and to connect eligible persons with needed support services.

PROFESSIONAL TRAINING

Digital Marketing Science, GreenFig University (2018) • Project Management Professional, Syracuse University (2017) • Lean Management, SimpliLearn, (2017) • Six Sigma Yellow Belt, Johns Hopkins Health System (2016) • Certified Federal Job Search Trainer/Certified Federal Career Coach, Federal Career Training Institute, (2014 & 2017)

BEFORE Federal Resume
2 Pages: Too Short, No Keywords, No Accomplishments

No military spouse mention

BOBBI ROBBINS

443-444-4444
email@gmail.com

Baltimore
MD 21228

OBJECTIVE: Family Readiness Officer, NF4, 4467

PROFESSIONAL SUMMARY

Basic summary; no metrics or other eye-catching info

Three years' experience as a Family Readiness Officer (FRO) and ten years of working with civilian families in a professional capacity. Continuously awarded highest possible ratings on performance reviews, willing to travel, able to maintain a flexible schedule to meet the needs of Marines, Sailors and their families. Seven years' experience with organizing and disseminating large amounts of data to students, families, Marines, and Sailors. Proficient in Microsoft (MS) Word, MS Excel, MS Outlook, MS PowerPoint, MS Publisher, Naval Correspondence, Adobe Acrobat and SharePoint.

EDUCATION

B.A. Asian Studies Major, University of Maryland University College, Okinawa, Japan, 2011

B.A. Psychology Major, **Human Development Minor**, State University of New York College at Geneseo, Geneseo, New York, 2008

WORK AND VOLUNTEER EXPERIENCES

Veteran and Federal Customer Services Representative   **Feb 2013 – present**

- Provide customer service to veterans, military spouses, and active duty service members as they search for federal and private sector employment.
- Connect customers with the resources to help with their job search.
- Quote customers on the cost and scope of work needed to make their resume competitive.

Family Readiness Assistant/Volunteer   **Jul 2009 – present**

- Provided organizational and communication aid to the Family Readiness Officers (FRO) for Combat Logistic Regiment 37, the 31st Marine Expeditionary Unit (MEU), and currently 3d Reconnaissance Battalion.
- Made telephone calls to welcome new families to the unit.
- Assist with quarterly newsletter publication for 3d Recon Battalion and monthly newsletters for the MEU.
- Help with the promotion and evaluation of unit events and workshops via spouse-based feedback.
- Assist with administrative duties such as reconciling rosters and service members' required documentation.

L.I.N.K.S. Mentor   **Feb 2012 – June 2013**

- Brief 1-2 assigned sections of the Lifestyle, Insight, Networking, Knowledge, Skills (L.I.N.K.S.) curriculum at monthly workshops of up to 40 participants.
- Coordinate appropriate activities to accompany oral instruction of L.I.N.K.S. materials.

CPR/AED/First Aid/Babysitters' Course Instructor   **Jul 2011 – June 2013**

- Teach cardiopulmonary resuscitation (CPR) and basic first aid to adults and teens in monthly classes of up to ten students as well as provide instruction on how to operate an automated external defibrillator (AED).
- Conduct monthly babysitters' classes to instruct up to 10 teens and pre-teens on how to properly care for infants and children.

Family Readiness Officer   **Nov 2009 – Jan 2013**

- Served at the battalion and regimental levels as the Commanding Officer's (CO) representative for Unit, Personal, and Family Readiness Program (UPFRP) outreach.
- Provided support and assistance to the Marines, Sailors, and their families through weekly informational email communications and newsletters, monthly target-specific educational workshops, and bi-annual family events.
- Used MS Excel, MS Outlook, and Marine Online to maintain distribution lists of up to 750 Marines spread throughout up to six companies and their family members; used distribution lists to facilitate home and section visits as well as telephone, post, and email communications in order to maximize awareness of the UPFRP and to connect eligible persons with needed support services.
- Coordinated the presence of program resource specialists at major unit events in order to increase accessibility.

- Conducted biannual surveys to assess needs of families and personnel in order to increase the program's value.
- Connected outbound personnel and family members with the FRO at their gaining command.
- Provided the CO with weekly informational updates on the UPFRP via email or brief and hosted monthly Command Team meetings for information dissemination and program activity coordination.
- Interviewed and supervised eleven Family Readiness Assistants and Command Team Advisors as well as coordinated annual volunteer recognitions from the CO and recognition at unit events.
- Utilized various software-based systems, such as SharePoint and resource websites, to gather resource information for inclusion in the weekly email; used MS Word to develop and publish a weekly newsletter that reflected this information and accompanied these emails; built and maintained the unit's eMarine website to serve as an additional reference point for current information.
- Managed annual Unit Family Readiness Funds budgets of up to $17,000, allocated funds and donated items and ensured that spending was within the guidelines stipulated for Non-Appropriated Funds.
- Fostered support systems for new and less experienced FROs through mentorship.
- Created marketing flyers and mailing postcards using MS Word and MS Publisher to promote awareness of targeted unit trainings and gatherings, such as pre-deployment briefs.
- Organized monthly workshops for families, such as the Okinawa Area Emergency Evacuation Plan brief, in order to increase readiness, resiliency and to encourage investment in the community.
- Organized quarterly workshops for Marines, such as Couples' Communication, as well as annual trainings, to include Understanding the UPFRP and Family Care Plan 101, in order to increase readiness and improve resource awareness.
- Provided extra support to families during the seven off-island exercises that required participation from the battalion and the regiment via briefs on available services and benefits and extra outreach.
- Coordinated with the FROs of the Camp Schwab units, MCCS Sponsorship, the Canine Unit, and other outside organizations in order to present the annual Do What Daddy Does event in support of the Month of the Military Child celebrations for more than 250 families; this event resulted in children and spouses having a better understanding and appreciation of their Marine/Sailor's job responsibilities.
- Coordinated with the FROs of 3d Marine Division and other outside organizations, such as the Camp Courtney Junior Marines, in order to present the first annual 3d Marine Division Marine Corps Birthday Ball for Kids.

Long lists of bullet statements make it very hard for HR Specialists to find the Knowledge, Skills, and Abilities that they are seeking

Possible accomplishment

Y.M.A.K. Institute   **Jul 2009 – Nov 2012**

- Developed lesson plans and conversational dialog examples in order to instruct 15 adult Japanese professionals in weekly conversational English and English grammar classes.
- Established an intensive English course for young adults in transition to overseas employment.
- Prepared monthly quizzes and motivated students to learn and practice English through interaction and discussion. These motivational practices increased student performance on quizzes and their understanding of the English language by 60% since July 2009
- The institute is still using the course material created.

Website Administrator and Newsletter Editor   **Aug 2010 – Jun 2012**

- Promoted the monthly Marine Officers' Spouse's Club of Okinawa events that supported the funding of local charities by updating the Facebook page, the website, and the newsletter.
- Created, edited, and distributed quarterly newsletters using MS Publisher and Homestead web hosting software.
- Obtained member-run business and outside organization advertisements to incorporate into the newsletter.
- Electronically distributed the quarterly newsletter to more than 300 members of the organization in order to increase participation in club events, present the quarter's charitable donations, and to maximize the amount of time that advertisers had their information on display.

Private Sector Resume
2 Pages: Bullet-style with Boldface Accomplishments

BOBBI ROBBINS
Baltimore, MD 21228 | 443-444-4444 | email@gmail.com

RELOCATION MANAGER | PROGRAM MANAGER

Optional: include military spouse mention here

Multifaceted professional with nine years of diverse experience with U.S. Military and private sector organizations in the U.S. and internationally. Cross-functional expertise in military relocation management, training and education coordination, and strategic workforce planning. Recognized throughout career for strong research, analytical, program management, project management, and stakeholder liaison, and customer service skills. Advanced technology skill set. U.S. Military Spouse. M.A.S. and B.A. degrees.

EXPERTISE SUMMARY

Program Management | Project Management | Client Retention | Customer Service/Relationship Management
Budget Management | Database Management | Team Leadership | Federal/Military Agency Liaison
Social Media: Facebook, LinkedIn, and Twitter

PROFESSIONAL EXPERIENCE

U.S. ARMY, Fort George G. Meade, MD (Additional locations in the U.S. & overseas)
Military Spouse Relocation Manager   5/2008 – Present

Military Spouse Summary Statement and PCS Military Spouse History

Manage all aspects of military family relocation, including transportation of goods, vehicles, pets, and family members. Served as Military Relocation Manager at the following installations: Fort George G. Meade, MD (7/2018 – Present; 7/2013 – 7/2016), Camp Pendleton, CA (7/2016 – 4/2018), Camp Schwab & Camp Kinser, Okinawa, Japan (5/2009 – 6/2013), and Marine Corps Base Quantico, VA (5/2008 – 5/2009).

- Coordinate move-in logistics and services, including location of home and registration at new installation for health, education, and family services. Coach personnel in cultural differences when moving abroad.
- Successful in helping military personnel successfully transition to new homes and assimilate in new locations.

THE RESUME PLACE, INC., Baltimore, MD
Program Manager / Certified Federal Job Search Trainer / Certified Federal Career Coach   1/2018 – Present

Training Program Manager: Manage webinar and in-person training programs for the Resume Place's "Ten Steps to a Federal Job" certification licenses. Coordinate communications, marketing, and relationship-building services with clients and senior-level government and military officials. Update annual training plans.

Training Program Instructor: Train career coaches and transition assistance professionals (TAP) in person and via webinars on helping military spouses navigate the Priority Placement Program-Spouses (PPP-S) and the benefits of the Military Spouse Program for securing federal positions.

Accomplishments are Included!

- Developed and leveraged strong partnerships with military base leadership and employment assistance personnel (EAP) to create effective training plans with measurable outcomes for Veterans, military spouses, college students and recent grads.
- Provided key research and edited new content for an upcoming update to *The Stars Are Lined Up for Military Spouses,* a book designed to support military spouses seeking federal jobs.

North County Health Services, San Marcos, CA
PROJECT & PLANNING MANAGER   10/2017 – 1/2018
PROGRAM PLANNING & GRANTS INTERN   6/2017 – 9/2017

Provided project leadership for a range of small and mid-sized projects. Built strong cross-functional relationships to ensure all stakeholders were appropriately engaged.

- Oversaw project timeline, budget, and implementation. Contributed to strategic and operational business plans. Tracked action items and provided status reports for projects.

BOBBI ROBBINS | 443-444-4444 | email@gmail.com | Page Two

JOHNS HOPKINS HEALTH SYSTEM, Baltimore, MD
Program Manager/Career Coach   8/2015 – 7/2016

Provided analytical, administrative, and technical support for the Johns Hopkins Health System, an organization that employs over 20,000 people annually. Assisted staff in the Office of Strategic Workforce Planning and Development (SWPD) with developing strategies to create pipelines to resolve staffing shortages for entry level personnel. Managed stakeholder engagement and supported strategic planning. Contributed to strategic planning.

- **Led team of internal and external stakeholders in development and launch of pilot training program for high school graduates** to address critical need for qualified Clinical Technicians. **8 students were accepted.**

- **Established structured, more efficient onboarding process for new Clinical Technicians** in the Nursing department's SOARING program. Led successful onboarding of 75 new hires in 3 cohorts. Developed aggregated assessment summaries for each candidate for the SOARING Team.

- **Created new desktop procedures manual** to support an on-site Career Coach at the Johns Hopkins Hospital, facilitating a smooth transition for new coaches with minimal disruption 800+ clients served.

- **Career Coach for 800+ entry- to mid-level employees seeking career counseling and job training**. Presented information sessions for internal career advancement. Administered skills assessments.

MARINE CORPS COMMUNITY SERVICES, Okinawa, Japan
Family Readiness Officer (FRO), Family Readiness Program (FRP)   11/2009 – 2/2013

Provided family members with resource information and support services to enhance personal and family readiness. Coordinated information, news, events, and activities. Represented the Command at conferences and meetings with high-ranking American and Japanese officials. Managed annual FRP budgets of up to $17,000.

- **Conducted biannual surveys** to assess needs of families and personnel to increase the program's value. Liaised with military leadership to advocate for support and services for military personnel and their families.

- **Wrote newsletters and email disseminated resource information**. Built and maintained a website.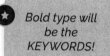

Bold type will be the KEYWORDS!

- Collaborated with local Okinawan resources and FROs across the 3d Marine Division to provide unit children with the first-ever Marine Corps Birthday Ball, connecting children to their service member parent's ethos.

EDUCATION

Master of Advanced Studies (M.A.S.), Leadership of Healthcare Organizations, 2017
University of California San Diego; GPA 3.9

Bachelor of Arts (B.A.), Asian Studies, University of Maryland University College (UMUC), 2011; GPA 3.82

Bachelor of Arts (B.A.), Psychology & Human Development, 2008
State University of New York at Geneseo; GPA: 3.34

TECHNICAL SKILLS PROFILE

Microsoft® Office Suite (Word, Excel, Outlook, PowerPoint, Access) • Adobe Connect • QuickBase • SharePoint • Gotomeeting.com• Google Docs • Weebly • WordPress • MailChimp • Constant Contact • QuickBooks • Google Analytics • Google Productivity Applications • Teamwork Project Management • Efforts to Outcomes (ETO) • Statistical Package for Social Sciences (SPSS) • Edmentum • e-Marine • Marine Online

SELECTED PROFESSIONAL TRAINING

Digital Marketing Science, GreenFig (2019) • Project Management Professional, Syracuse University (2017) • Lean Management, SimpliLearn, (2017) • Six Sigma Yellow Belt, Johns Hopkins Health System (2016)

Cover Letter
Target your cover letter to the job qualifications with keywords

Targeting this position:

Work and Family Life Consultant, NF 4, US Navy, Fleet & Family Support Program, Chinhae, South Korea

Target qualifications:

- ✪ **Financial Counselors** must possess a baccalaureate degree from an accredited college or a combination of education and experiences commensurate in serving as a PFM counselor. Must possess and maintain a nationally recognized financial counselor certification.

- ✪ Other positions require an Associate's degree or higher in education, social/behavioral, business administration, finance, economics, travel and tourism, marketing or related field. Experience providing **adult education** and/or work/family life consultation is preferred but not required.

- ✪ **Skill in conducting interviews** to establish the nature and extent of concerns and issues and provide assistance to develop goals and plans, in order to determine appropriate referral services and options.

- ✪ **Skill in preparation of presentations and public speaking** in personal-large and small group settings. Effective skill in forming and retaining working relationships with peers and leadership.

- ✪ **Skill in using various computer database, spreadsheet, word processing**, and network programs (e.g., as Internet, Microsoft Office Suite, and FFSP databases.

- ✪ Knowledge of the formulation and execution of **needs assessment tools**. Ability to communicate effectively in writing.

BOBBI ROBBINS

Baltimore, MD 21228 | 443-444-4444 | email@gmail.com

February 2, 2019

January Johansson
Fleet & Family Support Center,
Chinhae, South Korea
Box 22 PSC 111
FPO AA 96269

RE: WORK AND FAMILY LIFE CONSULTANT, Announcement 10202, Chinhae, South Korea

Dear Ms. Johansson:

I was excited to learn of the position of Work and Family Life Consultant in Chinhae, South Korea. We will be PCSing to South Korea in two months, and I would like to be considered for this position with my Military Spouse Preference, E.O. 13473.

My qualifications for the position include:

- **Financial Advisor** – Masters degree with courses in finance and business. Additionally, I am a current applicant for the FINRA Investor Education Foundation Military Spouse Fellowship to earn the Accredited Financial Counselor® credential and expect to have earned the designation before my arrival in South Korea.

- **Interviewer** – At Resume Place, as the Ten Steps to a Federal Job Certification Program Manager, I have interviewed class registrants regarding federal job search coaching and training interests, gathered their resume information, and provided training information.

- **Needs Assessment Interviewer** – I am experienced at survey, evaluation development, collection of information and reports design. I have used industry needs assessment programs to interview entry-level workers at Johns Hopkins Hospital to address their barriers to employment success.

- **Public Speaking / Instructor / Adult Education** – As a trainer for the Stars Are Lined Up for Military Spouses Program, I have presented the program at numerous military bases for spouses, military, and base staff.

- **Computers** – I am highly competent in Excel, Word, Quickbase (database), Quickbooks (accounting), and several social media systems.

I am available to interview by phone or Skype for the position. We will be arriving in South Korea in two months. I hope you will consider me for this position during our tour in South Korea.

Sincerely,

Bobbi Robbins

CASESTUDY

JAN MASON

Jobseeker Facts:

Active Duty Military Spouse

Solid Work History

Used E.O. 13473

Federal Employment Experience

Reinstatement

Photo: Jan helped establish the first Sesame Place room in Europe as a gathering place for moms and children. Photo credit: https://www.army.mil/article/60623/toddlers_parents_enjoy_sesame_street_makeover

Federal Career Objectives:

- ✪ GS-13/14
- ✪ Social Sciences, GS-0101
- ✪ Training Instructor or Curriculum Designer, GS-1702

Successful Federal Job Results:

- ✪ Hired - "I just wanted to let you know that I have a tentative job offer for the Training Specialist position based out of Fort Belvoir."

- ✪ "I've been working on my CCAR stories. It was a long process trying to gather/recollect this information, but a fun little trip down memory lane. I can definitely credit the accomplishment paragraphs and your practice interview phone call with me to aiding in the success of getting the job!"

"I went back and looked at the PPP matches. I had 22 matches, and out of those, ZERO referrals. The only positions I was referred for were ones that I applied for on my own. Of those, there were 16 applications total. I was not referred for 2 (due to veterans beating me out); contacted to interview for 6 (declined 3 of the interviews); accepted 3 interviews (was not selected from 2 of the interviews); had a second interview from the 1 interview and was ultimately selected for that position (NF04 Training Instructor)."

"I can definitely credit the accomplishment paragraphs and your practice interview phone call with me to aiding in the success of getting the job!"

CORRECT Military Spouse Federal Resume
5-Page; Outline Format with Accomplishments

JAN MASON
9400 Any Street • Anywhere, VA 22015
500-600-7777 • awesomespouse@yahoo.com

Authorized for Military Spouse Preference, EO 13473

E.O. 13473 right up front!

MILITARY SPOUSE WITH OVER 18 YEARS OF EXPERIENCE in Military Community Services and Family, Morale, Welfare and Recreation (FMWR). Strengths include staff development, budget administration, planning, team building, marketing, and customer service. Articulate communicator with outstanding interpersonal and analytical skills. Detail oriented and results driven; resourceful and effective organizational leader.

PCS History added to the Summary at the top

U.S. ARMY MILITARY SPOUSE PCS HISTORY

Dedicated U.S. Army Military Spouse with 16 years of experience of relocation of family and career to support U.S. Army Career Officer.

Jul 2017	Carlisle, PA	Jun 2007	Fort Leavenworth, KS
Jul 2017	Washington, D.C.	Jun 2006	West Point, NY
Jul 2015	Grafenwoehr, Germany	Dec 2002	Fort Sill, OK
Jul 2008	Wiesbaden, Germany	Mar 2002	Fort Lee, VA

HONORS AND AWARDS

Commander's Award for Public Service (2017)
IMCOM Stalwart Award (2015)
Superior Civilian Service (2015)
Army Community of Excellence Sustainment Award for USAG Wiesbaden (2014)
IMCOM ACS Center of Excellence Award (2014, 2012, 2011, 2009)
Army Community of Excellence Sustainment Award for USAG Wiesbaden (2012)
Army Community of Excellence (ACOE) Gold Award for USAG Wiesbaden (2011)
Achievement Medal for Civilian Service (2011)
Selected as Mentee for IMCOM Headquarters Centralized Mentoring Program (2010/2011)
IMCOM Commanding General Achievement Medal for Civilian Service (2010)
Commander's Award for Public Service (2006)

Honors and awards listed before work experience.

PROFESSIONAL EXPERIENCE

CONSULTANT   **10/2017–Present**
Federal Career Training Institute and The Resume Place, Inc.   10 hours per week
Catonsville, MD
Supervisor: Kathryn Troutman, 800-xxx-xxxx, may contact

Outline Format with Keywords

CONSULTANT AND TECHNICAL ADVISOR on military spouse and veteran employment for The Resume Place, a company specializing in Federal career consulting and training services, including federal resumes. Provide consultation on a broad range of topics, including the military spouse preference program, connecting with the local Family Service Center and a service's branch of Family Moral, Welfare and Recreation (FMWR), and other valuable services which are helpful to military families.

1

MARKETING AND COMMUNICATIONS: Author articles related to military spouse employment, which are featured on The Resume Place webpage. Provide coaching and consultation to individuals seeking federal employment.

SOLDIER AND FAMILY READINESS PROGRAM MANAGER, GS-0101-12 **07/2015–02/2016**
US Army DFMWR, Army Community Service   40 hours per week
USAG Bavaria, APO, AE 09114
Supervisor: Head Boss, 800-xxx-xxxx, may contact

MANAGED SOCIAL SERVICE PROGRAMS FOR U.S. MILITARY: Provided oversight and direction for six core program components of the Army Community Service (ACS) program, including Installation Army Volunteer Corps, Army Family Team Building program, Army Family Action Plan program, Mobilization and Deployment program, Employment Readiness program, and the Soldier & Family Readiness Center.

SUPERVISED SIX STAFF: Supervised five program managers in management of the six core installation Army Community Service (ACS) programs and one readiness center facility manager. Ensured subordinate program managers carried out ACS program functions in accordance with governing laws, policies, regulations, and professional standards of service. Reviewed the work of subordinates; accepted, rejected and amended work, as appropriate. Implemented changes in work assignments and work flow and balanced workload, as necessary, to increase the effectiveness of operations. Set performance goals and evaluated performance of subordinates.

DIRECTOR ARMY COMMUNITY SERVICE, GS-0101-13   **02/2009–07/2015**
US Army DFMWR, Army Community Service   40 hours per week
USAG Wiesbaden, APO, AE 09096
Supervisor: Mike Flip, 800-xxx-xxxx, may contact

DIRECTED ACS SOCIAL SERVICE PROGRAMS SERVING 19,000 PERSONNEL: Served as Army Community Service (ACS) Director and subject matter expert (SME) on programs supporting readiness for a geographically dispersed population of over 19,000 military personnel, family members, civilians, and retirees at Headquarters U.S. Army Europe (USAREUR), 5th Signal Command, 66th Military Intelligence Brigade, 1-214 Aviation Regiment, DODDS-Europe, and AAFES-Europe. Supervised 23 civilian employees and contractors.

MARKETING AND OUTREACH: Implemented outreach and managed social services programs to promote readiness for soldiers, families, retirees, and civilian employees. Specific programs included Financial Readiness and Education; Army Emergency Relief (AER); Relocation Readiness Program; Family Advocacy Program (FAP); Mobilization, Deployment and Support Stability Operations; Army Family Action Plan (AFAP); Army Family Team Building (AFTB); Exceptional Family Member Program (EFMP); Employment Readiness Program (ERP) New Parent Support; Survivor Outreach Services (SOS); Soldier and Family Assistance Center (SFAC); and Sexual Harassment/Assault Response and Prevention (SHARP).

DEVELOPED, INTERPRETED, AND APPLIED POLICIES, REGULATIONS AND PROCEDURES: Oversaw, developed, coordinated, and evaluated policies and procedures in support of the execution of ACS Programs. Supported commanders ensuring readiness through Financial Readiness Education, Relocation Readiness Program, EFMP, ERP, and FAP. Ensured programs were carried out in accordance with governing guidelines; relevant

2

legislation; budgetary policies; federal, state and host nation regulatory requirements; and professional standards of service.

PROGRAM ANALYSIS AND PROCESS IMPROVEMENT: Planned, directed, and evaluated ACS programs and developed recommendations and strategies to ensure optimum program achievement through ACS accreditation and self-evaluations. Conducted ongoing evaluations and assessments to identify program shortfalls and successes. Developed measures of effectiveness for ACS programs, including financial literacy training, FAP preventions and education training, readiness, and education.

DIRECTED, DEVELOPED, IMPLEMENTED, AND ADMINISTERED PLANS, PROCEDURES, AND REGULATIONS to provide a comprehensive soldier and family support program. Determined activities and services to be offered, initiated new programs, and modified or terminated existing programs. Ensured program modifications reflected real cost savings, efficiencies, or increased services. Analyzed all activities and programs for progress, problems, and trends to ensure they were operating efficiently and provided the best possible services. Based on findings, recommended changes to senior leadership.

BUDGET MANAGEMENT: Provided input for development of Program Objective Memorandum (POM) submissions to ensure the ACS center requirements were met. Ensured that resources were utilized in accordance with Army standards and programmed funding to meet the needs for service delivery.

HUMAN RESOURCES (HR) MANAGEMENT: Participated in the selection of key civilian staff members. Supported Equal Employment Opportunity (EEO) and worked closely with labor union representatives. Consulted with the HR Officer, CPAC Manager, and Management and Labor Relations Specialist to meet all personnel requirements and needs. Served as ACS and senior rater, as well as billing official. Applied knowledge of both CONUS and IMCOM Europe theaters, installations, their operations, and special circumstances they faced.

KEY ACCOMPLISHMENTS:

Accomplishments added to stand out!

LED ACS TO TOP PERFORMANCE: Following appointment as ACS Director in 2009, discovered USAG Wiesbaden had failed the previous Department of Army accreditation inspection and had taken months to meet standards for re-inspection. Set and clearly communicated two goals to my team: 1) to pass accreditation on first inspection and 2) to become the best ACS center in the Army. RESULTS: On our first inspection, we achieved 100% on all 207 standards and received Accreditation with Commendation. This perfect score was repeated three years later for the next inspection. Also achieved goal as the best ACS Center in the Army. Received the Army-wide "IMCOM Center of Excellence Award" in 2009, 2011, 2012, and 2014.

CREATED MARKETING STRATEGY, INCREASED PROGRAM VISIBILITY: Developed, promoted, and implemented fun, informative community events that were effective in increasing walk-in traffic and visibility of ACS services in a facility located away from the main base area. Some programs became so popular that they were expanded to other locations in Wiesbaden. RESULTS: Expanded community involvement drove a dramatic increase in size, number, and use of programs for family members and military, including employment and financial programs.

DELIVERED PRESENTATION TO 300+ GERMAN BUSINESS OWNERS at the Wiesbaden Chamber of Commerce on the challenges faced by military soldiers and families (such as

3

language barriers for soldiers and their family members) in order to promote partnership opportunities. RESULTS: Partnerships flourished with local tourism offices and two nearby cities. "English Spoken Here" signs were added in Wiesbaden businesses.

INNOVATED HIGHLY EFFECTIVE THREE-DAY "CULTURE COLLEGE PROGRAM" for new soldiers and spouses relocating to Germany to reduce the "intimidation factor" of going off base and adjusting to language differences. Provided orientation on local culture and customs, basic language instruction, and a city tour. RESULTS: The program was so popular, it was offered twice a month and attracted 80 attendees per session.

ESTABLISHED THE FIRST SESAME ROOM IN EUROPE: Garrison Wiesbaden's New Parent Support Program did not have space for services for families with infants and toddlers. Identified a vacant apartment in one of our buildings, submitted proposal to Sesame Street, and was awarded $5,000 to create a Sesame Room at our installation. The grand opening was attended by the Garrison Commander, media, and 50 guests.

The photo on the first page of this case study is from the grand opening of the first Sesame Street Room on a military base in Europe.

LAUNCHED A HOLIDAY FOOD BANK on base to support people in our community. Found space and oversaw a volunteer coordinator in collecting canned food donations for our annual "Make a Difference Day" project. The new volunteer-run Holiday Food Bank provided assistance to any ID card holder in our community. In the first year, 800 pounds of food were distributed to those in need.

ARMY VOLUNTEER CORPS COORDINATOR, GS-0101-11   **7/2008–02/2009**
US Army DFMWR, Army Community Service   40 hours per week
USAG Wiesbaden, APO, AE 09096
Supervisor: Sheila Dare, 800-xxx-xxxx, may contact

PLANNED, LED, AND COORDINATED PROGRAM OPERATIONS AND OUTREACH PRESENTATIONS: Recruited, trained, guided, and counseled volunteer staff and organizations. Served as the installation speaker for the Volunteer Program and as Chairperson of the Installation Volunteer Advisory Council.

FINANCIAL MANAGEMENT AND REPORTING: Served as Billing Official for ACS government purchase card accounts. Collected and submitted data for specific reporting requirements.

INTERPRETED AND APPLIED REGULATIONS AND POLICY: Applied and ensured compliance with HR, EEO, safety, inventory management, and internal control procedures, regulations, and policies. Assisted with passing USAG Wiesbaden ACS accreditation.

KEY ACCOMPLISHMENT:
Established the first Holiday Assistance and Angel Tree Programs at ACS to help military families experiencing financial hardships. Created program policies and procedures and led the planning. Managed collection and distribution of vouchers, gifts, and donations distributed to needy families. RESULTS: During tenure distributed holiday assistance to 998 families and 1,726 children, including over 1,000 toys and $16,500 in commissary gift cards.

4

EDUCATION

Master's Degree, Recreation Administration, University of North Texas, 1991
Bachelor of Arts, Advertising Art, University of North Texas, 1989

PROFESSIONAL TRAINING

Certified Federal Career Coach (2017)
Certified Federal Job Search Trainer (2017)
IMCOM ACS Director Training (2014)
IMCOM Academy Leadership & Mgmt for ACS Directors (2013)
IMCOM Academy Executive Leadership & Mgmt for FMWR Division Chiefs (2012)
Civilian Education System (CES) Advanced DL Course (2012)
Mentee in the IMCOM Headquarters Centralized Mentoring Program (2011)
7 Habits of Highly Effective Army Families Facilitator Training (2010)
FMWRC Survivor Outreach Services Training (2010)
FMWR Academy Special Events Course (2009)
FMWR ACS Instructor Training (2008)
MWR Academy Employment Readiness Program Manager's Course (2007)

ADDITIONAL INFORMATION

EARLIER CAREER EXPERIENCE:
ASSISTANT DIRECTOR COMMUNITY ACTIVITIES, GS-0301-12, 11/2000–08/2002
US Army MWR, 417th Base Support Battalion, Kitzingen, Germany (40 hours per week)

CHIEF OF SEMPER FIT, NL-0240-05, 02/1999–10/2000
Marine Corps Community Services, Camp Foster, Okinawa, Japan (40 hours per week)
- Provided leadership and guidance to program managers and 800 subordinate staff.
- Managed 153 recreation facilities and fields serving 50,000 military, civilian, and retired military personnel. Planned, managed, and executed Non-Appropriated Fund (NAF) operating and Appropriated Fund (APF) capital budgets.

RECENT VOLUNTEER EXPERIENCE:
- President, Bavaria Community and Spouses Club (2016–2017)
- Senior Advisor, 18th Combat Sustainment Support Battalion (2015–2017)
- Netzaberg Middle School Parent/Teacher Organization (2015–2017)

COMPUTER SKILLS: Microsoft Office Suite (Word, Excel, PowerPoint, Access), SharePoint, Google Productivity Applications

5

BEFORE Federal Resume
Hard-to-read big block federal resume

JAN MASON

9400 Any Street, Anywhere, VA 22015

500-600-7777, awesomespouse@yahoo.com

PROFILE: Accomplished leader with over 18 years of experience in Military Community Services and Family, Morale, Welfare and Recreation (FMWR) program management. Strengths include staff development, budget administration, planning, team building, marketing, and customer service. Articulate communicator with outstanding interpersonal and analytical skills. Detail oriented and results driven; resourceful and effective organizational leader.

WORK EXPERIENCE:

CONSULTANT (Telework)
The Resume Place, Catonsville, MD
10/2017-Current, Hours per week: 10
Duties, Accomplishments and Related Skills:
Serve as a Consultant and Instructor for The Resume Place with main area of focus being military spouse and veteran employment. Certified to teach "Ten Steps to a Federal Job", "The Stars are Lined Up for Military Spouses", and "Writing Your First Resume". Write articles related to spouse employment; provide coaching and consultation to individuals seeking federal employment.

> When we were coaching Jan to change her resume format from the Big Block style, she said, "The hardest part is getting away from the blocks of writing, but I'm getting there!"

COMMUNITY VOLUNTEER
USAG Bavaria, Grafenwoehr, Germany
07/2015 - 07/2017, Hours per week: 30
Duties, Accomplishments and Related Skills:
President of the Bavaria Community and Spouses Club: supervised 25 Volunteer Chairmen, and had highest membership at 230; responsible for club $60,000 operating budget; had oversight for philanthropy programs to include two Thrift Shops and their monthly operations; briefed Garrison Commander and community leaders at monthly Community Leaders Information Forum; Coordinated and coached the Netzaberg Middle School (NMS) Dodgeball Club; Parent Representative for the NMS School Advisory Committee; Senior Advisor to seven Family Readiness Groups in the 18th Combat Sustainment Support Battalion; Guest Speaker at local American's Working Around the Globe (AWAG) Conference; and Yearbook Committee volunteer for Netzaberg Elementary School.

SOLDIER AND FAMILY READINESS PROGRAM MANAGER (This is a federal job)
US Army DFMWR, Army Community Service
USAG Bavaria, APO, AE 09114
07/2015 - 02/2016, Hours per week: 40
Series: 0101 Pay Plan: GS Grade: 12
Duties, Accomplishments and Related Skills:

Supervised five program managers who managed six core installation ACS programs and one facility manager who managed a readiness center. The core program components included the Installation Army Volunteer Corps, Army Family Team Building program, Army Family Action Plan program, Mobilization and Deployment program, Employment Readiness program, and the Soldier & Family Readiness Center. Ensured that subordinate program managers carried out ACS program functions in accordance with governing laws, policies, regulations, and professional standards of service. Ensured that subordinate program managers published comprehensive standard operation procedures outlining program services and that such procedures were coordinated with other post elements. Reviewed work completed by subordinates, accepted, rejected and amended work as appropriate. Evaluated the effectiveness of operations supervised in terms of mission accomplishment, quality and quantity standards, procedural, policy and regulatory compliance, and technical competence. Made changes in work assignments and work flow and balanced workload as necessary which increased effectiveness of operations. Evaluated performance of subordinates.

DIRECTOR ARMY COMMUNITY SERVICE (This is a federal job)
US Army DFMWR, Army Community Service
USAG Wiesbaden, APO, AE 09096
02/2009 - 07/2015, Hours per week: 40
Series: 0101 Pay Plan: GS Grade: 13
Duties, Accomplishments and Related Skills:

★ *The "Center of Excellence" accomplishments are missing and definitely should be included.*

IMCOM Army ACS "Center of Excellence" award winner for 2009, 2011, 2012, and 2014. Successfully accomplished ACS Accreditation in 2011 and 2014 with zero deficiencies and 100% of possible points. Selected as Mentee for 2010/2011 IMCOM HQ Centralized Mentoring Program. Selected as Europe Region ACS Director representative to HQ IMCOM for development of ACS Strategic Plan.

Served as Army Community Service Director, and subject matter expert on programs. Implemented outreach and managed programs designed for identifying and resolving problems, and promoting readiness for Soldiers, Families, and civilian employees. Specific programs included Financial Readiness and education, Army Emergency Relief (AER), Relocation Readiness, Family Advocacy (FAP), Mobilization, Deployment and Support Stability Operations (Mob/Dep), Army Family Action Plan (AFAP), Army Family Team Building (AFTB), Exceptional Family Member Program (EFMP), Employment Readiness (ERP), New Parent Support, Volunteer Corps, Survivor Outreach Services (SOS), Soldier and Family Assistance Center (SFAC), and Sexual Harassment/Assault Response and Prevention (SHARP). Supported commanders ensuring readiness through Financial Readiness Education, Relocation Readiness Program, EFMP, ERP, and FAP. Ensured programs were carried out in accordance with governing guidelines; relevant legislation; budgetary policies; federal, state and host nation regulatory requirements; and professional standards of service. Monitored ACS program performance; developed recommendations, and techniques to ensure optimum program achievement through ACS Accreditation, and self-evaluations. Conducted on-going evaluations and assessments to identify program shortfalls and successes. Planned, directed, and evaluated the ACS programs and supervised a staff of 23 civilian employees and contractors. Championed employees by submitting them for awards, sending them to career development schools, professional training, and submitting them for promotions. Created, implemented, and facilitated staff training, goal setting, and team building exercises and events. Directed, developed, administered plans and procedures, and implemented regulations to provide for a comprehensive Soldier and Family support program. Determined activities and services to be offered; initiated new programs, and modified or terminated existing programs.

Ensured that program modifications reflected real cost savings, efficiencies, or increased services. Analyzed all activities and programs for progress, problems, and trends to ensure they were operating efficiently and provided the best possible services; based on findings, made appropriate recommendations to senior leadership. Interacted with all agencies and aspects of Family Programs to include Child and Youth Services (CYS), as well as various action officers and high senior ranking officials in European Region and IMCOM. Conducted General Officer level briefings and presentations. Managed QACS and OSD budgets and prepared 5-year AF/NAF budgets. Conducted ACS strategic planning, and served as SME on garrison strategic planning. Provided input for the development of POM submissions, to ensure the ACS center requirements were met. Ensured that the resources were in accordance with Army standards and funding was programmed to meet the needs for service delivery. Participated in the selection of key civilian staff members. Consulted with Human Resource Officer, CPAC Manager and Management and Labor Relations Specialist to assure that all personnel requirements and needs were met. Served as rater and senior rater. Monitored, tracked, and responded to customer feedback via the Interactive Customer Evaluation (ICE) system.

On numerous occasions acted as the Programs Director, Family and Morale, Welfare and Recreation (FMWR) for our medium garrison with full responsibility and managerial authority to plan and direct FMWR programs. The FMWR programs encompassed Nonappropriated Funds Resource Management Division, (NAF Financial Management, Marketing, Major Construction, Private Organizations, Commercial Sponsorship, Property Management, Internal Review and Management Controls, Supply, Warehouse and Maintenance, Public-Private Ventures, and Information Technology); Child and Youth Division, (Child Development Centers, Family Child Care, School Age Services, Youth Centers, Teen Centers, Youth Sports and Fitness, Youth Education Support -School Liaison-Outreach-Program Support Services); Recreation Division, (Sports and Fitness, Entertainment, Automotive, Parks and Picnic Areas, Library, Arts and Crafts, Community Activity Centers, Better Opportunities for Single Soldiers (BOSS), and Outdoor Recreation); and Community Business Division, (Clubs, Food and Beverage, Entertainment, Bowling, Golf, Recreation, Rod and Gun Clubs, Lodging Operations).

ARMY VOLUNTEER CORPS COORDINATOR (This is a federal job)
US Army DFMWR, Army Community Service
USAG Wiesbaden, APO, AE 09096
07/2008 - 02/2009, Hours per week: 40
Series: 0101 Pay Plan: GS Grade: 11
Duties, Accomplishments and Related Skills:
Ensured volunteers were recognized through formal and informal ceremonies. Served as the installation speaker for the Volunteer Program. Served as Chairperson of the Installation Volunteer Advisory Council. Maintained and updated the Volunteer Management Information System (VMIS) database. Recruited volunteers. Trained, guided, counseled volunteer staff and organizations. Served as Billing Official for ACS GPC accounts. Collected and submitted data for ISR and CLS reports. Experienced with NSPS, safety regulations, internal control procedures, inventory management, and EEO policies. Assisted with passing USAG Wiesbaden ACS Accreditation. Organized Garrison Holiday Assistance and Angel Tree Programs. Skilled at managing a full range of programs designed for resolving problems, working with multi-cultural customers, and promoting Soldier and Family readiness. Acted as ACS Director during the director's absence. Oversight for Financial Readiness Program, Family Advocacy Program, Relocation Readiness, New Parent Support, Information and Referral, Employment Readiness, Exceptional Family Member Program, Army Emergency Relief, Sexual Assault Response

Coordinator, Outreach, WTU, Army Family Team Building, Army Family Action Plan, and the Victim Advocate program.

EDUCATION:
University of North Texas Denton, TX
Master's Degree 08/1991
Major: Recreation Administration Minor: Business

University of North Texas Denton, TX
Bachelor's Degree 05/1989
Major: Advertising Art Minor: Recreation Administration

VOLUNTEER ACTIVITIES:
President, Bavaria Community and Spouses Club (2016/2017)
Senior Advisor, 18th Combat Sustainment Support Battalion (2015/2017)
Netzaberg Middle School Parent/Teacher Organization (2015/2017)
Volunteer, Hainerberg Elementary School Parent/Teacher Organization (2009-2014)
Volunteer, Wiesbaden Community Spouses Club (2010-2014)
Child Youth Services Sports (2012-2014)

AWARDS:
Commander's Award for Public Service (2017)
IMCOM Stalwart Award (2015)
Superior Civilian Service (2015)
Army Community of Excellence Sustainment Award for USAG Wiesbaden (2014)
IMCOM ACS Center of Excellence Award (2012)
Army Community of Excellence Sustainment Award for USAG Wiesbaden (2012)
IMCOM ACS Center of Excellence Award (2011)
Army Community of Excellence (ACOE) Gold Award for USAG Wiesbaden (2011)
IMCOM Commanding General Certificate of Achievement (2011)
Achievement Medal for Civilian Service (2011)
Selected as Mentee for IMCOM Headquarters Centralized Mentoring Program (2010/2011)
IMCOM Commanding General Achievement Medal for Civilian Service (2010)
IMCOM ACS Center of Excellence Award (2009)

> *The AWARD list is impressive! But the resume should include WHY she received these awards. What accomplishment or project resulted in these awards? Include the projects and accomplishments in the appropriate job block.*

CASESTUDY

ANN JONES

Jobseeker Facts:

Military Spouse, E.O. 13473

VEOA, 5 Point Veteran

VRA for positions up to GS-11

Had not been employed in 22 years

Photo: *Stars Are Lined Up for Military Spouses*, Joint Base Pearl Harbor, Honolulu, Hawaii, Summer 2018
Ann is furthest right, next to Kathryn Troutman

Federal Career Objectives:

- Administrative Assistant, GS-0301-06 through 09
- Protocol Officer, GS-0301-09/11
- Engineer, GS-0801-07

Successful Federal Job Results:

- HIRED with her first-ever federal resume for Administrative Assistant, GS-06, in the U.S. Air Force.
- Received another TENTATIVE job offer two months later for Secretary, GS-07, in the U.S. Navy.
- With this new federal resume, Ann is now applying to Protocol Officer positions, up to GS-11. She is getting REFERRED!

> *Ann said, "I went to the eTAP with my husband and I thought, why don't I look for a job too? But I haven't worked in 22 years!"*

CORRECT Military Spouse Federal Resume
4-Page; Outline Format with Accomplishments

ANN JONES   ajones@gmail.com

ANN JONES
Honolulu, HI 99999 US
Mobile: 577 777 7777
Email: gmailemail@gmail.com

Military Spouse – Authorized for E.O. 13473, Military Spouse Preference

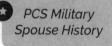

Authorized for E.O. 13473

Professional Summary

U.S. Army Military Spouse with 20 years of diverse professional experience. Proven experience in personnel and human resources, administrative operations, customer service, researching and interpreting laws and regulations, and technical project management. Skilled in use of automated systems, personnel document review, correspondence management, report and correspondence preparation. Prior U.S. Coast Guard experience as Assistant Program Reviewer, Human Resources Directorate. BS in Civil Engineering.

Military Spouse Summary Statement

Work Experience

U.S. Army Military Spouse/Volunteer   **Apr 1997 – Present**
Dates and Locations: 25 hours per week
Jan 2014 – Present   Pearl Harbor, HI
Nov 2010 – Dec 2013   Washington DC/Pentagon
Dec 2003 – Nov 2010   Yokosuka, Japan
Aug 2003 – Nov 2003   Newport, RI
May 2002 – Aug 2003   Washington, DC/Pentagon
Jan 2000 – Apr 2002   Monterey, CA
Jul 1998 – Dec 1999   Pascagoula, MS
Apr 1997 – Jun 1998   Charleston, SC

PCS Military Spouse History

MILITARY PERSONNEL DOCUMENT REVIEW: Experience in preparing documents, materials, and household goods for frequent moves throughout the U.S. and internationally. Prepare and correspondence and complete documents.

Outline Format with ALL CAPS KEYWORDS!

AUTOMATED SYSTEMS: Skill in utilizing automated systems for planning moves, tracking, and researching new locations and tracking expenses.

RESEARCHING AND INTERPRETING LAWS AND REGULATIONS: Familiar with military personnel laws and regulations regarding relocations, household good relocations, and family and medical services to support the military family. Respond to questions and provide advice.

MILITARY PROTOCOL KNOWLEDGE: Gained knowledge and experience in protocol operations and official social events with required logistics to meet the goals of the dignitary and our agency. Assist with logistics and cultural preferences for Distinguished Visitors and VIPs as they visited our military bases throughout our career. Co-plan official ceremonies and social events following proper protocol and social customs.

ANN JONES   gmailemail@gmail.com

Volunteer   **02/2014 – Present**
Military Chapel Center & Community Church   Hours per week: 20
1111 Center Street, Honolulu, HI 99999   **Supervisor:** Mrs. Mary Garner, 777-222-4444, May Contact

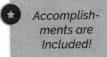
Volunteer experience is EQUAL to paid experience for federal HR reviews

Active volunteer supporting key areas and serving in a variety of different positions, including Women's Group Secretary, Lector Coordinator, Catechist, and Lay Minister.

SUPPORT ADMINISTRATIVE OPERATIONS AND COMMUNICATIONS LIAISON: Execute a wide range of administrative tasks for the Chapel Center. Type yearly calendar/agenda and various written correspondence to other organizations and sister groups. Track, monitor, and meet deadlines to ensure seamless daily operations. Respond to questions and provide advice from members, parishioners, and staff.

DATABASE MANAGEMENT: Use Microsoft® Office software and an automated database to maintain files; create correspondence; and produce reports, spreadsheets, newsletters, bulletins, and other written communications. Develop and maintain master roster spreadsheets, reports, name tags, the organization's email account, distribution lists, and social media accounts to reflect current membership, weekly volunteer lists, and other files for 50+ members. Prepare reports and summaries of budget, events, and objectives.

HUMAN RESOURCES AND TRAINING: Prepare weekly lesson plans to teach Catholic Doctrine as a religious education teacher to students varying in ages from 3–14 for Vacation Bible School and Sunday Catholic Religious Education. Class sizes average 10–15 students. Over 45 children successfully received required religious sacraments on time.

DEVELOP PLANS AND CONDUCT TRAINING as Lector Coordinator for 25+ adult personnel to standardize lector procedures for military parish community. Coordinate weekly schedule of lectors for weekly Sunday mass and daily mass resulting in more streamlined and uniform execution of lector delivery and presentation. Respond to questions and provide advice.

EVENT PLANNING, COORDINATION, AND EXECUTION: Plan, organize and coordinate special events, including events to attract new members, board meetings, and charity events. Coordinate and oversee set up of reception table. Assist other board members with weekly meetings, fellowship set up, and other arrangements such as audio/visual presentation aids, brochures, decorations, refreshments, and guest speakers or meetings with 50+ attendees

Key Accomplishments:

Accomplishments are Included!

- PLANNED AND ORGANIZED EFFECTIVE EXHIBITS AND EVENTS FOR NEW MEMBER RECRUITMENT that generated 10+ new members. As a result, membership is at an all-time high at 50+ members.
- ORGANIZED MULTIPLE CHARITY EVENTS serving the local military and homeless in need and community service organizations. Cultivated a supportive environment to strengthen community bonds. Organized three events to feed more than 60 homeless men.

- DESIGNED, CREATED, AND MAINTAINED PARISH'S FIRST WEEKLY BULLETIN, which included a comprehensive Parish Directory, updates, and announcements from all parish departments and interest groups; general announcements; upcoming events; and important dates. Reviewed and edited all submissions for proper grammar, spelling, and punctuation. Carefully crafted bulletins using graphic designs and appropriate clipart using MS Office and document design software. Praised by parish leaders and community.

- DESIGNED AND CREATED INFORMATION CARDS AND BANNERS for production, distribution and display for the Women's Church Group to recruit new members and advertise the group's calendar of events and studies for the year. Designed user-friendly map and driving directions to the chapel center. Received excellent feedback from users and new members for creating top quality and effective communications.

Delivery Order Manager/Project Manager   **08/1995 – 02/1996**
Engineering Services Corporation   Hours per week: 40
2100 Revenue Drive, Houston, TX 77001   **Supervisor:** Ann Ivy, 555-888-1111, May Contact

Early career in engineering!

TECHNICAL PROJECT MANAGEMENT: Drafted and developed planning design for on-post minor construction improvement and renovations projects (less than $60K). USED AUTOMATED SYSTEMS for planning and design.

RESEARCHED AND INTERPRETED REGULATIONS: Ensured design and safety code requirements were met. Managed and oversaw projects, timeline, completion, and quality assurance by civilian subcontractors as approved by Engineering Facilities Managers. Worked with Government Engineering Facilities Managers on project design proposals.

Coast Guard Officer   **05/1989 – 06/2003**
U.S. Coast Guard Pay and Personnel Center   Hours per week: 40
444 S.E. Quincy St., Topeka, KS 66683   **Supervisor:** Admiral George Prongs, 711-111-1111, May Contact

Military Experience, Veteran, 5 points

Held diverse leadership positions over 14 years across multiple operational areas, including Personnel and Human Resources (HR), Administration, Operations, Logistics, Safety, and Law Enforcement. Supervised, trained, and led as many as 45 personnel and managed budgets of up to $70K.

COMMANDING OFFICER of a 110' Patrol Boat, Freeport, TX: Oversaw personnel, material condition, safety, performance and safe navigation. Supervised 15 personnel, managed $70K annual budget. Trained crew for newly commissioned ships.

ASSISTANT PROGRAM REVIEWER, Human Resources Directorate, USCG Headquarters, Washington, DC: On team that reviewed UCG HR Directorate programs. Drafted reports, reviewed and analyzed data, recommended program enhancements, resource proposals, and decision memos to streamline initiatives and reduce costs.

INTELLIGENCE WATCH OFFICER/ASST SENIOR RESERVE OFFICER/RESERVE ADMIN SUPERVISOR, USCG Pacific Area (Pi), Alameda, CA. Supervised diverse work groups, responsible for detection, monitoring, analysis and dissemination of tactical intelligence information for to all area units and commands. PERFORMED ROUTINE ADMINISTRATIVE TASKS. Arranged unit member lodging and travel to meet training and qualification requirements for advancement.

OPERATIONS OFFICER/OPERATIONS DEPARTMENT HEAD, High Endurance Cutter, Charleston, SC: Supervised 45 personnel, managed $65K annual budget. Collected, compiled, and disseminated information. Scheduled and coordinated logistics and clearances for port visits.

Key Accomplishment:

- TECHNICAL COMPETENCE / REGULATORY RESEARCH AND INTERPRETATION: Selected as representative for the Engineering and Acceptance Trial Board, Accepted Vessel and Assumed Command. Developed, implemented and maintained Ship Organization and Regulations Manual. During vessel boardings, ensured compliance with applicable federal laws and regulations. Provided technical guidance to all levels of personnel.

Education

U.S. Coast Guard Academy, New London, CT
Bachelor's Degree, Civil Engineering. 05/1989

U.S. Military Honors and Awards

Commendation Medal
Achievement Medal

BEFORE Federal Resume
3 Pages: Not Targeted

MRS. Ann I Jones
Honolulu, HI 99999 US
Mobile: 5777777777
Email: gmailemail@gmail.com

Ann worked on this original USAJOBS federal resume with the Military & Family Support Center JBPHH. This resume WORKED, She was hired for her first application for her first position in government!

Availability:
Job Type: Permanent, Term, Telework
Work Schedule: Full-Time, Part-Time

Desired locations:
United States - HI - Honolulu

Work Experience:
Military Chapel Center & Community Church
1111 Center Street, Bldg 1790
Honolulu, HI 99999 United States

02/2014 - Present
Hours per week: 20
Volunteer, Women's Group Secretary, Lector Coordinator, Catechist, Lay Minister,
Duties, Accomplishments and Related Skills:

ADMINISTRATION:
• Scheduled meetings, recorded, typed and distributed minutes of monthly board and council meetings and executed administrative tasks to include typing yearly calendar/agenda and various written correspondence to other organizations or sister groups, tracked and met deadlines to ensure seamless daily operations
• Developed and maintained master roster spreadsheets, reports, name tags, organization's email account, distribution lists and social media accounts to reflect current membership, weekly volunteer sign-up lists, and other appropriate files; total membership of 50+
• Designed, created and maintained parish's first weekly bulletin, which included a comprehensive Parish Directory, updates and announcements from all parish departments and interest groups; general announcements, upcoming events and important dates; reviewed and edited all submissions for proper grammar, spelling, punctuation, word usage and relevance; carefully crafted bulletins using graphic designs and appropriate clipart using MS Office and document design software programs; praised by parish leaders and community
• Designed and created Women's Church Group Information cards and banners for production, distribution and display in order to recruit new members and advertise the group's calendar of events and studies for the year; designed user-friendly map and driving directions to chapel center; hailed by users and new members

EVENT PLANNING/PUBLICITY:
• Planned and organized exhibits and events to recruit new members. Over 10 new members recruited; membership at an all time high at 50+ members
• Organized charity events serving local military and homeless in need and community service organizations alike; cultivated a supportive environment to strengthen community bonds. Organized 3 events to feed more than 60 homeless men
• Coordinated and oversaw reception table set up and assisted other board members with weekly meetings and fellowship set up and other arrangements, such as audio/visual presentation aids, brochures, decorations, and refreshments, to accommodate 50+ attendees, to include guest speakers

HUMAN RESOURCES/TRAINING:
• Prepared weekly lesson plans to teach Catholic Doctrine as a religious education teacher to students varying in ages from 3-14 for Vacation Bible School and Sunday Catholic Religious Education (CCD). Average class sizes: 10-15 students. Over 45 children successfully received required religious sacraments on time
• Developed plans and conducted training as Lector Coordinator for 25+ adult personnel to standardize lector procedures for military parish community. Coordinated weekly schedule of lectors for weekly Sunday mass and daily mass resulting in more streamlined and uniform execution of lector delivery and presentation
Supervisor: Mrs. Mary Garner ((777) 222-4444)
Okay to contact this Supervisor: Yes

U.S. Coast Guard
U.S. Coast Guard PPC
444 S.E. Quincy St
Topeka, KS   66683-3591 United States

05/1989 - 06/2003
Hours per week: 80
Coast Guard Officer
Duties, Accomplishments and Related Skills:

LEADERSHIP, ADMINISTRATION, OPERATIONS AND PROJECT MANAGEMENT,
PUBLIC RELATIONS, PERSONNEL MANAGEMENT, LOGISTICS, INTELLIGENCE, LAW
ENFORCEMENT, PUBLIC SAFETY

• ASSISTANT PROGRAM REVIEWER. USCG Headquarters, Washington, DC (G-CPA)
(Office of Programs). Team member reviewing U.S. Coast Guard programs of the
Human Resources Directorate. Drafted reports, reviewed and analyzed data,
provided recommendations for program enhancements, resource proposals, billet
reprogramming, and decision memos to streamline initiatives and reduce costs.

• INTELLIGENCE WATCH OFFICER/ASST SENIOR RESERVE OFFICER/RESERVE
ADMIN SUPERVISOR USCG Pacific Area (Pi), Alameda, CA. Supervised diverse work
groups, responsible for detection, monitoring, analysis and dissemination of tactical
intelligence information for to all area units and commands. ADMIN: Responsible for
routine administrative tasks. Training Coordinator; arranged unit member lodging
and travel to meet training and qualification requirements for advancement

• OPERATIONS OFFICER of 378' High Endurance Cutter. USCGC DALLAS, Charleston,
SC Operations Department Head for collection, evaluation & dissemination of
combat, tactical & operation information for cutter mission assignments; supervised
45 personnel, managed $65K annual budget. Scheduled and coordinated all ship
port visits, logistics arrangements & port visit clearances. Executed operations
command, control and communications to include 2 major drug seizures with an
estimated street value of over $4M. Hand selected to represent the Commanding
Officer during high-profile Community Relations visit to Haiti; escorted and
conducted ship tour and provided operational briefing on Humanitarian Relief
efforts and progress to Haitian President Preval and U.S. Ambassador Swing. Other
duties: Senior Watch Officer, Command Security Officer. Personal Award: CG
Commendation Medal

Education:
U.S. Coast Guard Academy New London, CT United States
Bachelor's Degree 05/1989

Major: Civil Engineering

CASE**STUDY**

NATALIE GORDON

Jobseeker Facts:

Eligible for E.O. 13473

Fluent in three languages

Over 20 years of experience as a foreign language instructor, translator, and interpreter

Photo: Natalie gets to try to make kimchee during a volunteer kimchee-making event in Korea.

Federal Career Objectives:

⚙ Preparing to PCS again and searching for a position as a foreign language instructor, translator, or interpreter.

Successful Federal Job Results:

⚙ Natalie entered our contest and had the opportunity to have a free rewrite of her federal resume. See it in this case study.

WINNER OF THE MILITARY SPOUSE FEDERAL RESUME WRITING CONTEST!

Natalie's Award-Winning Response

This is Natalie's actual contest write-up about her job as a Military Spouse! This is wonderful and inspiring. She has had a GREAT career as a military spouse. It's time for a new career now that her husband is retiring in a few months.

My current duties as a Military Spouse include but are not limited to:

- Primary caregiver and emergency contact for our 2 children, ages 19 and 13;
- POC for any repairs in our government housing unit;
- CFO of the household, in charge of paying all the bills and making minor financial decisions. (my husband has equal voting rights on the major decisions);
- Chief Communications Officer: providing and ensuring smooth communication with family members, children's schools, husband's work (as needed), movers, packers, utility providers, landlords, insurance companies, banking institutions, etc.;
- Cleaning Crew Chief: assigning, delegating, supervising and/or carrying out various cleaning projects as needed;
- Chief Planning Officer, in charge of scheduling and keeping track of all deadlines and appointments, particularly those pertaining to the upcoming move. Also in charge of acquiring, wrapping and mailing all the gifts for friends and family.
- Activities Director: in charge of suggesting activities for family, maximizing the cultural benefits of being in Korea and organizing said activities.
- Chef: planning, shopping for and cooking family meals, as well as food for holiday gatherings with single/unaccompanied airmen, husband's work potlucks and cook-offs, and community events.

Additional Duties:

- Part-time ESL teacher at Army Community Services;
- PTSO board member at the Seoul American Middle High School;
- Air Force Key Spouse for the 303 IS Det 1

Job Challenges:

My main challenge being a Military Spouse is finding a job that utilizes my two Master's degrees, especially overseas, where military spouses are severely limited by the positions available on their respective bases/posts and/or SOFA agreement restrictions. I am one of the lucky few, actually working in one of the fields I majored in, even though it's part-time. Being a single parent to two young children during my husband's deployments and TDYs, with our families thousands of miles away, was extremely hard as well. I learned some really hard lessons: there was only so much of me to go around; it was OK to ask for help; things didn't have to be perfect; kids really needed rules and routines; TV news was declared taboo for the sake of everyone's sanity during my husband's deployments to Iraq.

Cross-Cultural Challenges

Korean social and cultural norms are very different from what we are used to in Western society. Greeting people, handling a bill at a restaurant, professional relationships- everything is a challenge. I tried to do some research before we came to Korea, and after we arrived in Seoul, enrolled in beginner Korean classes on base. This turned out to be the best decision ever: not only did I make some new friends in class who showed me around Seoul, but our Korean teacher also turned out to be a treasure trove of Korean cultural knowledge. She organized the most amazing outings for our class and introduced us to her friends, such as a traditional hanbok-maker. She designs traditional Korean outfits following using authentic materials and techniques. I am learning to appreciate and understand Korean culture. The Korean language still presents a challenge, though!

Target Job Title: Foreign Language Instructor

Minimum Qualifications:

- Bachelor's degree in one of the following fields or related studies: **Education, Foreign Languages, Linguistics**.
- **Native-like fluency** in one of the languages listed above, as well as advanced English proficiency (applicants will be required to take proficiency tests in their claimed language).
- Demonstrated knowledge of the **respective area's history, culture, politics and economy**.
- Ability to use the latest technology and teaching techniques.

Desired Qualifications:

- Experience **teaching language skills to adult learners**, taking them from beginner level to the general **professional proficiency in an intensive setting**.
- **Experience living, working and/or studying abroad**.

Education:

- Bachelor's degree in one of the following fields or related studies: **Education, Foreign Languages, or Linguistics**.
- GPA of at least 3.0 on a 4.0 scale.

Keywords for the Outline Format Federal Resume:

- FOREIGN LANGUAGES – NATIVE-LIKE FLUENCY
- LINGUISTICS
- TEACHING LANGUAGE SKILLS TO ADULT LEARNERS
- PROFESSIONAL PROFICIENCY IN INTENSIVE SETTING
- LIVING, WORKING, AND STUDYING ABROAD

CORRECT Military Spouse Federal Resume
Outline Format with Accomplishments

NATALIE GORDON
APO, AP 96204
(010) 777-8888
email51@hotmail.com

MILITARY SPOUSE: Authorized for EO 13473, Military Spouse Preference ● ——— *E.O. 13473 right up front!*

OBJECTIVE: Foreign Language Instructor, Interpreter, Translator

SUMMARY OF QUALIFICATIONS

Foreign Language Instructor, Translator/Interpreter, and USAF Military Spouse with 20+ years of experience with living, working, and studying abroad. Advanced foreign language and cross-cultural communication skills.

- Multilingual: Fluent in German, English, and Russian; some conversational Italian and Spanish.
- In-depth knowledge of the history, culture, politics and economy of Germany, Italy, and South Korea.
- Experience includes teaching language skills to adults and elementary, middle and high school students from diverse linguistic and cultural backgrounds.
- Ten years as a translator and writer for multinational corporations, small businesses, and nonprofits. Skilled in using the latest technology and teaching techniques to enhance classroom learning, increase student engagement, and achieve language proficiency goals.

EDUCATION

- Bachelor's and Master's degree in Applied Linguistics, Translation, and Interpreting (German, English, Spanish, Russian); Minor in Economics; University of Saarland, Germany
- Bachelor's and Master's degree in Foreign Languages (English/German) with teaching expertise, Novosibirsk State Pedagogical University, Russia

WORK EXPERIENCE

United States Air Force Military Spouse / Volunteer   **9/1997–Present**
United States, South Korea, Italy, and Germany   25 Hours Per Week

USAG Yongsan, South Korea	Jul 2017–Present
Pentagon, VA	Oct 2014–Jun 2017
NSA Naples, Italy	Oct 2011–Oct 2014
Nellis AFB, North Las Vegas, NV	Aug 2009–Oct 2011
Bolling AFB, Washington, D.C.	Jul 2008–Jul 2009
Hickam AFB, Honolulu, HI	Aug 2005–Jul 2008
Brooks City Base, San Antonio, TX	Jul 2003–Jul 2005
Vogelweh, Kaiserslautern, Germany	Sep 1997–Jul 2003

Military Spouse PCS Military Spouse History as a job block

My current duties as a Military Spouse include but are not limited to:

CHIEF COMMUNICATIONS OFFICER: Providing and ensuring smooth communication with family members, children's schools, movers, packers, utility providers, landlords, insurance companies, banking institutions, etc.

1

NATALIE GORDON   (010) 777-8888 | email51@hotmail.com

CHIEF PLANNING OFFICER: In charge of scheduling and keeping track of all deadlines and appointments, particularly those pertaining to moving. Property and financial manager for household. Assign, delegate, and supervise cleaning projects.

EVENTS MANAGER: Suggest and organize activities for family to maximize the cultural benefits of being in Korea. Plan holiday gatherings with single/unaccompanied airmen, work potlucks and cook-offs, and community events.

- **Volunteer / Key Spouse, 303 Intelligence Squadron, Detachment 1, Seoul, S. Korea,** 11/2017–present (4 hours per month): Lead liaison between military family members and the detachment's leadership. Attend quarterly training for Key Spouses. Forward important information to military spouses. Attend military functions open to family members as well as family events.

ENGLISH AS A SECOND LANGUAGE (ESL) TEACHER   03/2018–Present
Army Community Services, US Army, Seoul, South Korea   Hours per week: 2
Supervisor: John Smith, jsmith@comcast.net, may contact   Salary: $20/hour

TEACH ENGLISH LANGUAGE SKILLS TO ADULT LEARNERS: Provide English language instruction to 7–10 adult foreign language nationals using approved ESL curriculum. Teach two classes per week to primarily Korean native speakers with varying levels of English proficiency.

LEVERAGE LINGUISTICS SUBJECT MATTER EXPERTISE AND NATIVE-LEVEL FLUENCY IN ENGLISH to improve the English language skills of my students from beginner level to general proficiency in an intensive classroom setting.

Outline Format with Keywords

APPLY KNOWLEDGE OF THE LATEST INSTRUCTIONAL METHODOLOGIES to meet the highly-customized needs and specific challenges of students. Incorporate the latest technology and adapt teaching methods and instructional materials to meet students' needs and learning styles.

DRAW ON EXPERIENCE LIVING, WORKING, AND STUDYING ABROAD, including more than a year living and working in Yongsan, South Korea, to connect with students. Model respect for the customs and culture of the country. Demonstrate knowledge of the area's history, culture, politics, and economy.

TRANSLATOR / FREELANCE COPYWRITER   07/2015–Present
Neonway.com (German software developer)   Hours per week: 2–5
Neonway, Siemensstr.14, D-64289 Darmstadt, Germany   Salary: $18/hour
Supervisor: Warren Fitt +49 (0) 123-456-789-29, may contact

MULTILINGUAL WRITER AND TRANSLATOR for Neonway.com, a German software developer that creates apps for a wide range of operating systems, including smartphones.

DEMONSTRATE NATIVE-LIKE FLUENCY IN FOREIGN LANGUAGES: Leverage fluency in English and German to create video tutorials for Neonway apps and product descriptions for the AppStore and the company's website. Create business correspondence and public relations releases about the apps in German and English.

2

NATALIE GORDON   (010) 777-8888 | email51@hotmail.com

LINGUISTICS PROFESSIONAL: Developed advanced linguistics skills and fluency in German through intensive academic study at the University of Saarland, Germany, where I earned a Master's degree in Applied Linguistics, Translation, and Interpreting (German, English, Spanish, Russian). Also hold a Master's degree in Foreign Languages (English/German) from the Novosibirsk State Pedagogical University, Russia.

FREELANCE INTERPRETER/TRANSLATOR / TRANSCRIBER   **05/1995–09/2006**
Multiple German Multinational Corporations/Nonprofits   Hours per week: 3-6
Landstuhl, Germany (and other cities in Germany)   Salary: $18/hour

NATIVE-LIKE FLUENCY IN GERMAN: Served as an Interpreter, translator, and transcriber for German and international companies.

- SAP/Contractor, Walldorf, Baden-Württemberg (11/2003–12/2006): Transcribed international business conferences for SAP, a multinational software corporation with regional offices in 180 countries.
- Freelance Translator, Import-Export Ort, Landstuhl, Germany (07/1998–06/2003): Translated business correspondence, financial documents, as well as various technical documents for a small business in Landstuhl, Germany.
- Freelance Interpreter, Otto Benecke Stiftung, e.V (05/1995–12/1996): Served as an Interpreter for a nonprofit run by the German Ministry of Education. Interpreted at educational seminars for young immigrants. Provided information about German courses, language school curriculum, and other language-course related issues.

ADDITIONAL VOLUNTEER EXPERIENCE

Seoul American Middle High School PTSO, Executive Board Member/Secretary, Seoul, S. Korea, 8/2018–Present; 7 hours/month
- Participate at board meetings as well as General Membership meetings; prepare minutes of the meetings; volunteer at school functions.

American Forces Spouses' Club, Seoul, S. Korea, 8/2017–5/2018; 10 hours/month
- As a Ways & Means Committee member, helped raise funds for the organization by selling merchandise at monthly luncheons.
- As a Luncheon Committee member, planned luncheons, purchased decorations and decorated the ballroom where luncheons were held. Named Volunteer of the Month in 11/2017.

Naples Overseas Support Club, Executive Board Member/Secretary; Thrift Store Volunteer, Naval Support Activity (NSA), Naples, Italy, 08/2012–10/2014; 25–30 hours/month
- As a board member/secretary, participated in board meetings, kept minutes, volunteered at the organization's functions. As a thrift store volunteer, helped raise funds for the organization. Named Volunteer of the Month, 5/2014.

3

BEFORE Federal Resume

Natalie Gordon
APO, AP 96204
(010) 7777-8888
email51@hotmail.com

Natalie's before resume is barely a resume. It is far too short for EITHER a private sector or federal resume.

OBJECTIVE
A full-time or part-time position utilizing my language skills.

SUMMARY OF QUALIFICATIONS
- 10+ years translation experience working with small businesses and nonprofit organizations
- Hands-on experience with international cultures as well as culturally diverse groups of people
- Experience teaching ESL to elementary, middle and high school students as well as adult foreign nationals

EDUCATION
- Master's degree in Linguistics, Translation and Interpreting (German, English, Spanish, Russian), Minor in Economics, University of Saarland, Germany, 2002
- Master's degree in Foreign Languages (English/German) and the teaching thereof, Novosibirsk, Russia, 1994

WORK EXPERIENCE
- **Part-time ESL teacher, Army Community Services, Seoul, South Korea**
  March 2018-present
  Provide classroom instruction for adult foreign nationals using approved ESL curriculum, as well as addressing specific challenges English presents to mainly Korean native speakers. 2hrs/week
- **Freelance copywriter/Translator, Neonway.com (a German software developer)**
  2015-present
  Create video tutorials for Neonway apps, as well as app descriptions for AppStore and the company's website, handle business correspondence and PR for the apps.
- **Freelance transcriber, SAP through a contractor**
  2003-2006
  Transcribed international business conferences for SAP, a German software company.
- **Freelance Translator, Import-Export Ort**
  1998-2003
  Translated business correspondence, financial documents as well as various technical documents for a small business in Landstuhl, Germany.
- **Freelance Interpreter, Otto Benecke Stiftung, e.V (nonprofit run by the German Ministry of Education)**
  1995-1996
  Interpreted at educational seminars for young immigrants providing information about German courses, language school curriculum and other language-course related issues.

- **Secretary/Interpreter/Office Manager, JPB Import**   1992-1994
  Planned and coordinated meetings, staff training, multilingual travel arrangements and business correspondence for a small business in Novosibirsk, Russia.
- **Intern/Part-time English Teacher, General Education School #12**
  Taught English to elementary, middle and high school students in Novosibirsk, Russia

VOLUNTEER EXPERIENCE

- **Air Force Key Spouse for 303 Intelligence Squadron, Detachment 1, Seoul, S. Korea**   November 2017-present
  Serve as a liaison between military family members and the detachment's leadership; attend quarterly training for Key Spouses; forward important information to military spouses, attend military functions open to family members as well as family events.

- **Seoul American Middle High School PTSO Executive Board Member (Secretary)**   August 2018-present
  Participate at board meetings as well as General Membership meetings; prepare minutes of the meetings; volunteer at school functions.

- **American Forces Spouses' Club volunteer, Seoul, S. Korea**
                                                    August 2017- May 2018
  As a Ways & Means Committee volunteer, helped raise funds for the organization by selling merchandise at monthly luncheons. As a Luncheon Committee member, helped plan luncheons, purchase decorations and decorate the ballroom where luncheons were held. Was named Volunteer of the Month in Nov.2017

- **Naples Overseas Support Club Executive Board Member/Secretary, Thrift Store Volunteer, Naples, Italy**   2012-2014
  As a board member/secretary, participated in board meetings, kept minutes, volunteered at the organization's functions. As a thrift store volunteer, helped raise funds for the organization. Was named Volunteer of the Month in May 2014.

Cover Letter
Outline Format with Accomplishments

Targeting this position:

Training Instructor, GS-1712-9, US Navy, US Pacific Fleet

Target qualifications:

For the GS-09: One year of specialized experience equivalent to the next lower grade level (GS-07) or pay band in the federal service or equivalent experience in the private or public sector **preparing lesson plans and providing classroom instruction in the practical application of trades theories, practices and technical requirements.**

Education

If you are using education to meet all or part of the qualification requirements, you must submit a copy of your transcripts or an **itemized list of college courses which includes equivalent information from the transcript (course title, semester/quarter hours, and grade/degree earned) in your resume.**

When the application process is complete, we will review your resume to ensure you meet the hiring eligibility and qualification requirements listed in this announcement. You will be rated based on the information provided in your resume and responses to the Occupational Questionnaire, along with your supporting documentation to determine your ability to demonstrate the following competencies:

- **CREATIVITY AND INNOVATION**
- **DEVELOPING OTHERS**
- **ORAL COMMUNICATION**
- **TRAINING PROGRAM ADMINISTRATION**
- **WRITTEN COMMUNICATION**

NATALIE GORDON

APO, AP 96204 | (010) 777-8888 | email51@hotmail.com

February 23, 2019
Human Resources Recruiter
US Navy EIC
San Diego, CA

Re: Training Instructor, GS-1712-09, San Diego, CA

To whom it may concern:

I am interested in the position of Training Instructor in San Diego. I am a military spouse, and we will be relocating to San Diego in three months. I would like to be considered with Military Spouse Preference, E.O. 13473. My qualifications for the position are the following:

- **EDUCATION** – BS and MS in Linguistics and Instruction
- **CREATIVITY AND INNOVATION** – First, I am creative and innovative in my teaching and translating experiences. My goal is to ensure that my students LEARN! Additionally, as a military spouse accompanying my husband to 8 locations in the last 20 years, I have demonstrated creativity in our successful moves internationally with my family.
- **DEVELOPING OTHERS** – As an interpreter, translator, and teacher, I continuously work to develop others in their area of expertise to improve their learning and communications skills.
- **ORAL COMMUNICATION** – As an ESL teacher for the ACS in Seoul, South Korea, I am skilled in instruction for students and professionals.
- **TRAINING PROGRAM ADMINISTRATION** – Developed instructional materials with adult learning systems for numerous topics as an ESL teacher and translator.
- **WRITTEN COMMUNICATION** – I am skilled as a writer of curriculum, instruction, evaluations, and communications.
- **COORDINATION** – As a military spouse and volunteer on all of our military bases, I have become adept in coordination of programs and projects. I am organized and efficient with logistics, events, and teams.

I am available for interview by Skype or telephone. I will be arriving in San Diego in May 2019. Thank you for your consideration.

Sincerely,

Natalie Gordon

Attachments: PCS Orders, Marriage Certificate, College Transcripts

CASE**STUDY**

JENNIFER P

Federal Career Objectives:

Retirement is on the horizon for her service member spouse. Jennifer has five years left as a military spouse, PLUS five children to put through college!

Successful Federal Job Results:

- ✪ **Successful federal job applicant** with PPP-S and USAJOBS—landed a GS-07 position as a Management Assistant

- ✪ **December 2018 Update:** Jennifer has finished her MBA and has a new position now as a Contract Specialist (GS-1102), GS-09 with promotion potential to GS-12. She could be a GS-12 by 2020.

Jobseeker Facts:

Eligible for E.O. 13473
Recent graduate
Relocating CONUS
First-time federal applicant

"I am looking for some assistance with building my federal resume and tips for the application process. I hope to increase my chances for receiving an offer. I just completed my Bachelor's degree and plan to pursue my MBA in the spring. I would like a position that promotes career advancement and professional growth."

CORRECT Military Spouse Federal Resume
5 Pages; Outline Format with Accomplishments

Jennifer P
Warner Robins, GA 31088 US
(404) 111-1111 | fedjobseeker@gmail.com

Authorized for Military Spouse Preference, EO 13473, Robins AFB

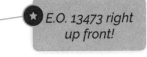

E.O. 13473 right up front!

CAREER OBJECTIVES: Human Resources Series, GS-0201; Administrative and Program Series, GS-0301; Accounting and Budget, GS-0500.

SUMMARY OF SKILLS: Military Spouse and recent graduate with a B.A. in Business Administration. Performance-driven, detail-oriented achiever with exemplary organizational and time management skills; able to consistently meet deadlines. Specialized experience with Human Resources, specifically in payroll, benefits, and training. Proficient in managing accounting procedures and ensuring accurate cash transactions and record keeping.

PCS History added to the Summary at the top

UNITED STATES AIR FORCE MILITARY SPOUSE PCS ORDER HISTORY:

- Robins AFB, Warner Robins, GA   2016–Present
- Kadena AFB, Okinawa, Japan   2011–2016
- Kirtland AFB, Albuquerque, NM   2005–2011

EDUCATION

BACHELOR OF ARTS DEGREE IN BUSINESS ADMINISTRATION   06/2012–07/2016
Ashford University, Forbes School of Business, Clinton, IA 52732
GPA: 3.97 of a maximum 4.00, Honors: Summa Cum Laude

Highlighting recent education by listing before work experience

Developed and honed skills in all areas of business. Communication courses aided understanding of dynamics of interpersonal relationships. Examined verbal and nonverbal communication patterns between people in personal, social, academic, and professional settings, and evaluated the nature of those interactions using contemporary communication theory. Learned to identify my own interpersonal communication behaviors and how to critically evaluate and improve oral communication skills. Managerial finance courses strengthened my ability to assess and determine the decisions and actions needed to improve the long-run performance of a company, including environmental scanning, strategy formulation, strategy implementation, and evaluation and control.

ACADEMIC RESEARCH PAPERS AND CASE STUDIES:

- Strategic Management & Business Policy: Course required a case analysis of Porsche Holding, which included a description of the company's history, products, and major competitors. Assessed financial performance and condition of the organization, conducted SWOT analysis detailing the strengths, weaknesses, opportunities, and threats that may affect the organization. Evaluated company decisions made and provided recommendations for improvement.

- Organizational Behavior: This research paper required the identification of components that contributed to organizational conflict and how to successfully address them in a team environment. I identified and assessed the source(s) and level of the conflict and provided evidence to support my findings, then described the steps I proposed to resolve the conflict and provided 3 possible conflict outcomes that could reasonably occur as a result of the conflict resolution.

➢ RELEVANT COURSEWORK: Business management, human resource management, accounting, economics, managerial finance, interpersonal communication, business communication, statistics for managers, visual literacy for managers, intro to computer applications, analytical writing, and technical writing. Core classes required 10-page reports, which included extensive research, data collection, and writing analysis. Utilized Microsoft Office software programs to communicate and present findings to peers and professors through various mediums such as PowerPoint, research papers, and speeches.

➢ GRADUATE LEVEL COURSES:
- *Management Communication with Technology Tools:* Emphasis was on technology, theories and models, qualitative communication research methodologies, and research writing.
- *Organizational Behavior:* Investigated behavioral factors that affect modern organizations and their management. Topics included group and team dynamics, organizational structure, motivation, leadership, power, and change management.

PROFESSIONAL EXPERIENCE

RECORDS ASSISTANT/ HUMAN RESOURCE ASSISTANT   **09/2010–10/2011**
Brown Mackie College-Albuquerque   Hours/Week: 40
10500 Copper Ave, Albuquerque, NM 87123 United States
Supervisor: Tonya Rhett, (803) 585-5555; May contact

RECRUITMENT AND PLACEMENT SUPPORT: Conducted new hire orientation and training. Answered employee questions relating to payroll, benefits, and other various Human Resource-related topics. Assisted with special events and projects such as student open house, annual benefits enrollment, etc. Utilized the Human Resource Information System (HRIS) database to keep contact information up-to-date and generate scheduled or requested reports.

STUDENT, PERSONNEL, AND ACCREDITING AGENCY RECORDKEEPING: Updated and maintained academic files for over 300 current and former students. Created, updated, and maintained personnel and accrediting agency files for over 50 employees.

★ Outline Format with Keywords

OFFICE AUTOMATION SOFTWARE: Utilized Education Management Corporation (EDMC) office automation software to provide Registrar and Human Resource services as they related to clerical and administrative support functions. Entered student attendance, course registration, and course scheduling; input final grades and populated attendance reports. Processed and entered incoming high school and college transcripts, and submitted college transcripts for transfer credit review through the college's system.

ORAL AND WRITTEN COMMUNICATION: Utilized oral and written communication to provide customer service to students, faculty, staff, and external inquiries in person, over the telephone, and through email correspondence. Distributed daily attendance reports to management and highlighted the students whose absences increased their probability for course failure or drop out.

★ Accomplishments added to stand out!

ACCOMPLISHMENTS: Achieved zero errors on personnel and accrediting files during the Accrediting Council for Independent Colleges and Schools (ACICS) inspection. Contributed to the zero errors on student academic files for the Registrar Department during ACICS inspection.

JENNIFER P   (404) 111-1111 | fedjobseeker@gmail.com

RECEPTIONIST   01/2010–09/2010
Brown Mackie College- Albuquerque   Hours/Week: 40
10500 Copper Ave, Albuquerque, NM 87123 United States
Supervisor: Steve Sampson, (505) 336-3333; May contact

VERBAL AND WRITTEN COMMUNICATION: Greeted persons entering establishment, determined nature and purpose of visit, and directed or escorted them to specific destinations. Generated and mailed student acceptance letters and reminders to new students and maintained copies in permanent academic files. Provided excellent customer service while operating an eight-line telephone switchboard to answer calls, respond to public inquiries, and communicate needed information.

RECORD KEEPING: Generated permanent academic and financial aid student files daily, and managed computer-generated records. Verified all records adhered to state, federal and accreditation regulations. Prepared and distributed daily and weekly reports to Admissions regarding future class start information.

OFFICE AUTOMATION SOFTWARE AND EQUIPMENT: Tracked student academic placement testing scores for Admissions Department through an electronic document management system. Transmitted information or documents to customers by phone, email, mail, or facsimile. Utilized system to maintain a current record of staff members' availability and current location.

TRAINING: Trained all part-time receptionists on front office duties. Assisted new Admission Advisors with accurately completing new student enrollment documents.

ACCOMPLISHMENTS: Designed and created all front office documents used to sign in guests and log and disseminate all phone and online inquiries to Admissions Department. Shared office documents with a newly opened affiliated school's front office staff to assist in their transition.

CERTIFIED SHIFT MANAGER   02/2009–01/2010
CiCi's Pizza Buffet   Hours/Week: 40
4770 Montgomery Blvd NE D104, Albuquerque, NM 87109 United States
Supervisor: Andrew Groves, (505) 668-2424; May not contact

MANAGEMENT: Managed a team of up to 15 employees per shift. Oversaw all areas of the restaurant and made final decisions on matters of importance to guest service in absence of the General Manager. Scheduled employee shifts and made adjustments when needed. Resolved guest complaints, taking appropriate action to turn dissatisfied guests into return guests. Resolved interpersonal conflict between employees and/or shift managers.

RECRUITMENT AND TRAINING: Interviewed potential employees and made recommendations to General Manager for final decision. Trained and provided direction to employees regarding operational and procedural requirements or issues in order to maintain product quality and cleanliness. Retrained employees who did not meet the standard or transferred them to a position where they did excel.

OFFICE AUTOMATION: Utilized restaurant's Pizza Point of Sale (POS) system to track inventory levels and order goods if levels were low or if sales forecasts predicted an increase in current week's future sales. Managed employee labor to reduce labor costs. Ran financial reports at end of each business day to compare them to the cash received and credit card sales. Operated POS system to input customer orders or issue refunds.

AFFILIATIONS
Sigma Beta Delta Honor Society – Awarded to business students in the top 20% of their class.
Golden Key International Honour Society – Awarded to Bachelor's degree-seeking students in the top 15% of their undergraduate class based on GPA.
Alpha Sigma Lambda Honor Society – Awarded to students in online programs seeking their Bachelor's degree and in the top 20% of students based on GPA.

- 3 -

BEFORE Federal Resume
Bulleted federal resume; not targeted to announcement

Jennifer P
Warner Robins, GA 31088

OBJECTIVE

A performance-driven achiever with exemplary organizational and time management skills, along with a high degree of detail orientation is seeking an entry level to mid-level management position within a company that promotes career advancement and professional growth.

EDUCATION

ASHFORD UNIVERSITY-FORBES SCHOOL OF BUSINESS   **Clinton, Iowa**
B.A. Business Administration, July 2016
➤ Summa Cum Laude
➤ Graduate courses:
    ❖ BUS 600- Management Communications with Technology Tools
    ❖ BUS 610- Organizational Behavior

PROFESSIONAL EXPERIENCE

Brown Mackie College   **Albuquerque, New Mexico**
Records Assistant/Human Resource Assistant   *Sep 2010 – Oct 2011*
➤ Updated and maintained academic files for over 300 current and former students
➤ Entered student attendance and distributed attendance reports to management on a daily basis
➤ Assisted in student orientation, registration, course scheduling, inputted final grades, and preparation for next quarter
➤ Processed incoming high school and college transcripts, and submitted college transcripts for transfer credit review
➤ Created, updated and maintained personnel and accrediting agency files for over 50 employees
➤ Achieved zero errors on personnel and accrediting files from Accrediting Council for Independent Colleges and Schools (ACICS) inspection
➤ Contributed to the zero errors on academic files for the Registrar Department during ACICS inspection
➤ Conducted new hire orientation, and answered employee questions relating to various payroll, benefits and HR issues
➤ Assisted with special events and projects such as student open house, annual benefits enrollment, etc. as needed
➤ Provided customer service to students, faculty, staff, and external inquiries at the Registrar window and over the telephone

Brown Mackie College   **Albuquerque, New Mexico**
Receptionist   *Jan 2010 – Sep 2010*
➤ Greeted persons entering establishment, determined nature and purpose of visit, and directed or escorted them to specific destinations
➤ Generated all permanent academic and financial aid student files as well as computer generated records daily
➤ Verified all files created adhered to state, federal and accreditation regulations
➤ Designed and prepared all front office documents used to sign in guests and track phone and online website inquiries
➤ Generated student acceptance letters and reminders
➤ Tracked student academic placement testing scores for Admissions Advisors
➤ Transmitted information or documents to customers using computer, mail, or facsimile machine
➤ Kept a current record of staff members' availability and current location
➤ Generated and mailed all letters to incoming students and maintained copies in permanent academic files
➤ Assisted the Admission advisors with preparing for each new start date with new student listing and student badges
➤ Prepared and distributed daily and weekly reports to Admissions regarding future class start information
➤ Trained part time receptionists on all front office duties
➤ Operated telephone switchboard to answer, screen, or forward calls, provided information, and took messages

CiCi's Pizza Buffet   **Albuquerque, New Mexico**
Certified Shift Manager   *Feb 2009 – Jan 2010*
➢ Managed a team of up to 15 employees per shift
➢ Oversaw all areas of the restaurant and made final decisions on matters of importance to guest service in absence of the General Manager
➢ Scheduled employee shifts and made adjustments when needed
➢ Resolved guest complaints, taking any and all appropriate actions to turn dissatisfied guests into return guests
➢ Maintained product quality and cleanliness
➢ Trained and provided direction to employees regarding operational and procedural requirements or issues
➢ Allocated the accurate amount of money to each register before assigning an employee to it
➢ Completed morning bank deposit and obtained adequate cash and change for the business day
➢ Maintained registers by skimming drawers hourly to deter and minimize internal and external theft

McDonalds   **Albuquerque, New Mexico**
Shift Manager   *Nov 2007 – Feb 2009*
➢ Managed a team of 15-20 employees per shift to ensure quality of service
➢ Supervised personnel to ensure that employees were following proper safety and food preparation procedures
➢ Tracked store's inventory and
➢ Verified monies in safe and registers to ensure that the accurate amount is accounted for and documented in system
➢ Trained and developed team members' skills and placed them in areas where they excelled
➢ Allocated the accurate amount of money to each register before assigning an employee to it
➢ Maintained registers by skimming drawers hourly to deter and minimize internal and external theft
➢ Updated employee time sheets and food safety logs

United States Army   **Fort Jackson, South Carolina**
Administrative Specialist   *Jan 2001 – Mar 2004*
➢ Greeted visitors or callers and handled their inquiries or directed them to the appropriate person according to their needs
➢ Operated multi-line phone system and provided information to callers, took messages, and transferred calls
➢ Updated and maintained paper and electronic filing systems for records, correspondence, and other material
➢ Composed, typed, and distributed meeting notes, routine correspondence, and reports
➢ Maintained scheduling and leave for unit personnel
➢ Ordered and dispensed unit supplies
➢ Distributed incoming mail or other materials and responded to routine letters

SKILLS

➢ Interpersonal Communication
➢ Intercultural Awareness
➢ Time Management
➢ Adaptability
➢ Leadership
➢ Organizational Skills
➢ Client relations

AFFILIATIONS

➢ Member of Sigma Beta Delta Honor Society
➢ Golden Key International Honour Society
➢ Alpha Sigma Lambda Honor Society

PART03

Hiring Programs and Authorities

"A two-income home will allow my family to weather financial storms due to emergencies and provide additional income to allow us to save since it never fails to rain."

As you take the journey of being a military spouse on the federal job hunt, there's plenty to discover. The more you can learn about federal jobs, the better. There are different types of federal positions, a variety of hiring categories, a broad range of benefits, and a number of application classifications and processes. As you dive into this strange world of federal hiring, remember: the more you know, the better your odds. This is because the more you know, the more options you'll realize you have. For example, your first federal job could be a "competitive service" position. But, later, you might apply for an "excepted service" position. Lately, "NAF" positions (which are funded through other sources than Congressional appropriations) have become popular because of changes in congressional budget processes. Derived Preference for military spouses is a powerful hiring authority that could be a game changer in your job search. And PPP-S is another special hiring program for DoD jobs that have different requirements you need to know.

There's a lot learn! So let's get started and look at some of these key pieces to your military spouse job search strategy.

Hiring path

Select all

- ☑ Open to the public (1219)

Federal employees (2390)
- ☑ Competitive service (765)
- ☑ Excepted service (169)
- ☐ Internal to an agency (459)
- ☐ Career transition (CTAP, ICTAP, RPL) (806)
- ☐ Land & base management (191)

Armed forces (1262)
- ☐ Veterans (715)
- ☑ Military spouses (482)
- ☐ National Guard & Reserves (65)

Students & recent graduates (116)
- ☐ Students (94)
- ☐ Recent graduates (22)

Senior executives (58)
- ☐ Senior executives (58)

Additional paths (1339)
- ☐ Individuals with disabilities (530)
- ☐ Family of overseas employees (158)

E.O. 13473 Hiring Paths for Military Spouses

Competitive and Merit Positions	Military spouses may apply for positions open to "Federal Employees" and positions open to "U.S. Citizens" (if they are U.S. citizens).
Excepted Service	Some positions or agencies fall under Excepted Service, which are sometimes temporary positions ranging from one to four years and provide the same benefits and promotion opportunities as Merit and Competitive federal positions.
Nonappropriated Funds (NAF)	NAF jobs are available on all military bases with the same benefits as General Schedule (GS) federal jobs. Many positions are with the Morale, Welfare, and Recreation activities.
Derived Preference	Family members may utilize a military member's 10 point preference for special consideration.
Program S (Priority Placement Program)	Eligible military spouses may apply for federal jobs at Department of Defense (DOD) agencies with benefits for application placement and priority.

Competitive and Merit Promotion Positions

Military spouses can apply to both kinds of federal jobs posted on USAJOBS

- ✪ "Open to the Public (US Citizen)" jobs are competitive positions.
- ✪ "Federal Employee" jobs are merit promotion positions.

Open to the Public (US Citizen) jobs are competitive

- ✪ Anyone with U.S. citizenship may apply. You will be competing with other members of the general public.
- ✪ You can apply for these jobs if you've never worked for the federal government (or don't have civil service "status").
- ✪ Veterans' preference does apply to these positions.
- ✪ This is the normal entry route into the civil service for most employees.
- ✪ The selecting official may fill the job from outside the civil service or from among candidates with civil service status.

Federal Employee jobs are Merit Promotion positions

- ✪ These announcements are limited to current or former federal employees. You will be competing against other "status" candidates.
- ✪ You will not be competing with members of the general public!
- ✪ Veterans' preference does not apply to these positions.
- ✪ To limit your USAJOBS search to "Merit Promotion" positions, select the "federal employee filter." Also, read the "Who May Apply" section of the job announcement. It will typically state "status candidates" or "merit promotion." Other groups (such as those who may be hired under special hiring authorities) may also be listed - such as military spouses!

Program S and E.O. 13473 military spouses apply for "federal employee" announcements that meet the Program S requirements (e.g., DOD CONUS jobs within commuting distance of your PCS) and match their series/grades. But they may also decide to apply for U.S. Citizen vacancies.

Sample job announcement: "Who May Apply"

Who May Apply: This includes employees on career or career-conditional appointments, individuals eligible for special appointing authorities such as Veterans Employment Opportunity Act, Interagency Career Transition Program/Career Transition Program, Schedule A, and individuals on Interchange Agreements with Other Merit Systems. (such as Military Spouse EO 13473)

Competitive vs. Excepted Service

Federal jobs are split into two types of service. The two types of jobs can even be found at the same agency, such as at NASA.

COMPETITIVE SERVICE:
Information Technologist

- Competitive Service jobs are subject to OPM's hiring rules, pay scales, etc.
- Traditional competitive hiring process applies
- Can earn tenure a.k.a. "status" over time
- Status allows you some hiring benefits
- Cannot be easily fired
- Earn raises according to a formula of time served
- Open jobs must be posted online
- Must compete for the job with the general public

EXCEPTED SERVICE:
Astronaut

- Excepted Service jobs are excepted from the requirements of the civil service laws or from competitive service by statute or regulation. These appointments are used in cases when it is not feasible to use qualification standards, competitive examinations, or competitive procedures
- OPM places positions in the excepted service under Schedules A, B, C, or D
- Cannot earn "status"
- Are hired at-will, more like private industry
- Can earn raises according to performance
- May be hired or fired for special reasons
- Open jobs do not have to be publicly announced and most are not posted on USAJOBS
- Do not have to compete for your job with the general public

Examples of Excepted Service Positions

These positions are in the excepted service. Employment in the excepted service does not confer competitive status to apply to competitive service jobs in the federal civil service.

The position expiration date (not to exceed date) may be extended based on workload and funding availability and is not subject to regulatory time limits.

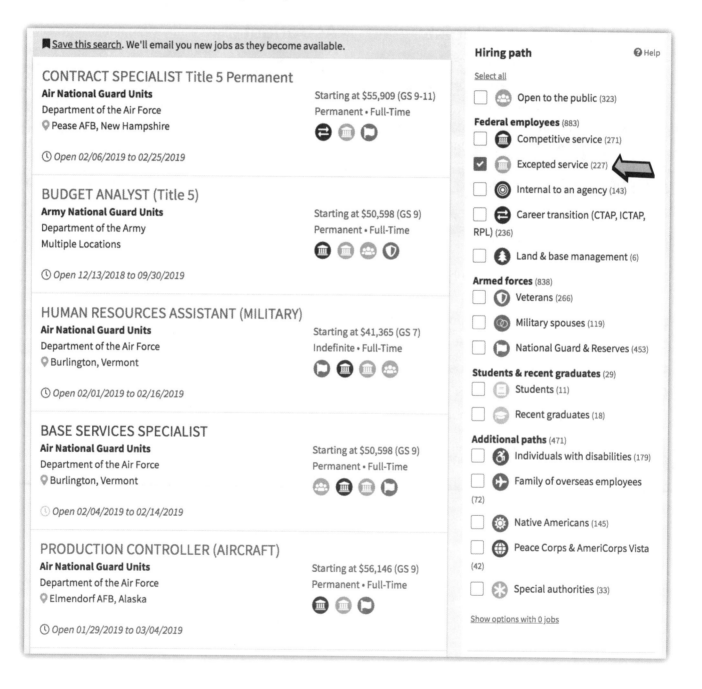

🔖 Save this search. We'll email you new jobs as they become available.

CONTRACT SPECIALIST Title 5 Permanent
Air National Guard Units
Department of the Air Force
📍 Pease AFB, New Hampshire
Starting at $55,909 (GS 9-11)
Permanent • Full-Time

🕐 Open 02/06/2019 to 02/25/2019

BUDGET ANALYST (Title 5)
Army National Guard Units
Department of the Army
Multiple Locations
Starting at $50,598 (GS 9)
Permanent • Full-Time

🕐 Open 12/13/2018 to 09/30/2019

HUMAN RESOURCES ASSISTANT (MILITARY)
Air National Guard Units
Department of the Air Force
📍 Burlington, Vermont
Starting at $41,365 (GS 7)
Indefinite • Full-Time

🕐 Open 02/01/2019 to 02/16/2019

BASE SERVICES SPECIALIST
Air National Guard Units
Department of the Air Force
📍 Burlington, Vermont
Starting at $50,598 (GS 9)
Permanent • Full-Time

🕐 Open 02/04/2019 to 02/14/2019

PRODUCTION CONTROLLER (AIRCRAFT)
Air National Guard Units
Department of the Air Force
📍 Elmendorf AFB, Alaska
Starting at $56,146 (GS 9)
Permanent • Full-Time

🕐 Open 01/29/2019 to 03/04/2019

Hiring path ❓ Help

Select all

☐ Open to the public (323)

Federal employees (883)
☐ Competitive service (271)
☑ Excepted service (227)
☐ Internal to an agency (143)
☐ Career transition (CTAP, ICTAP, RPL) (236)
☐ Land & base management (6)

Armed forces (838)
☐ Veterans (266)
☐ Military spouses (119)
☐ National Guard & Reserves (453)

Students & recent graduates (29)
☐ Students (11)
☐ Recent graduates (18)

Additional paths (471)
☐ Individuals with disabilities (179)
☐ Family of overseas employees (72)
☐ Native Americans (145)
☐ Peace Corps & AmeriCorps Vista (42)
☐ Special authorities (33)

Show options with 0 jobs

Sample Job Block for Excepted Service Resume: Social Worker

SOCIAL WORK INTERN
VA Palo Alto Health Care System
Palo Alto, California
Supervisor: XXXXX; May be Contacted.

XXXX to XXXX
30 hours/week
Salary: XXXX stipend

GRADUATE FIELD PLACEMENT INTERNSHIP working in the inpatient psychiatry unit at VA Palo Alto Health Care System.

PLANNED DIRECT CLINICAL SERVICES AND TREATMENT for Veterans of diverse cultures who were diagnosed with depression, PTSD, and other affective disorders with a range of time since initial diagnosis. Provided ongoing clinical services, including one-on-one counseling and therapy with Veterans, support for families, and establishing community-based services for care beyond discharge from the inpatient setting. Assessed psychosocial functioning, conducted psychosocial assessments, short-term treatment plans, case management, and assisted in the discharge of clients.

PERFORMED INITIAL DIAGNOSTIC EVALUATIONS. Acknowledged for my skills in completing comprehensive psychosocial assessments in a thorough and goal-oriented manner. Knowledge of medical terminology and mental health diagnoses, disabilities and treatment. Implemented psychosocial treatment and performed supportive problem solving and crisis interventions and upheld procedures for Veterans in inpatient psychiatry. Assessed need for continued treatment and disposition of patients.

COMMUNICATION AND COLLABORATION. Worked extensively with Veterans, family members, informal and formal care providers, and the operators of Residential Care Facilities. Coordinated placements in facilities including skilled nursing and long-term locked facilities. Established clear communication with Veterans, family members, friends, and other professionals. Collaborated with interdisciplinary team members on a weekly basis and/or daily basis on the progress of the client and to achieve project/program goals. Participated in weekly clinical supervision and group training and consultations. Provided consultation services to primary care providers, psychiatrist, therapist and/or other staff on psychosocial needs of client.

REFERRED CASES within VA Substance Abuse Programs to other clinicians when indicated. Adept at consulting with, coordinating with, and referring to community-based service organizations (e.g., federal/state/local social services agencies). Provided community resources and made appropriate referrals to assist clients in their area of living.

KEY ACCOMPLISHMENTS:
- I was the primary clinician for an older Veteran with two suicide attempts in a short period of time. In addition to his suicidal ideation and impulse control issues, he was grappling with substance abuse and extended grief. I collaborated with the Veteran, family members, psychiatrist, and psychologist to set up a full range of psychiatric services and group therapies. I conducted extensive research on community resources and assisted him in identifying volunteer opportunities and classes. He was very interested in teaching others and I found an opportunity for him to do so at a local library. As a result of my efforts, the Veteran connected not only with the VA, but built community connections and activities for his future orientation.
- Together with another intern, I designed and taught weekly psycho-education groups grounded in evidence-based practice (EBP).

NAF Jobs

NAF jobs are funded by the installation rather than through the Congressional appropriation process.

NAF employment is considered federal employment. It is, however, different from federal civil service employment because the monies used to pay the salaries of NAF employees come from a different source. NAF money is generated by activities such as Morale, Welfare, and Recreation (MWR) Programs and other activities that use NAF employees.

Army
www.USAJOBS.gov
Search: "NAF Army"

Navy
www.navymwr.org/jobs/ and USAJOBS
On USAJOBS, search: "NAF Navy"

Air Force
www.nafjobs.org/viewjobs.aspx
On USAJOBS, search "NAF Air Force"

Marine Corps
www.usmc-mccs.org/careers/ (click on Prospective Employees under Job Search & Apply); on USAJOBS, search "NAF USMC"

Sample Navy NAF Jobs

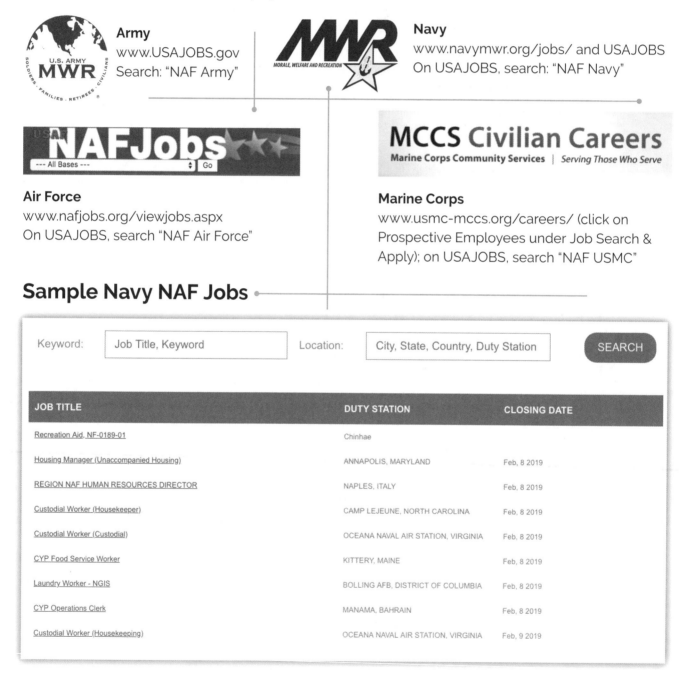

Keyword: [Job Title, Keyword]   Location: [City, State, Country, Duty Station]   [SEARCH]

JOB TITLE	DUTY STATION	CLOSING DATE
Recreation Aid, NF-0189-01	Chinhae	
Housing Manager (Unaccompanied Housing)	ANNAPOLIS, MARYLAND	Feb, 8 2019
REGION NAF HUMAN RESOURCES DIRECTOR	NAPLES, ITALY	Feb, 8 2019
Custodial Worker (Housekeeper)	CAMP LEJEUNE, NORTH CAROLINA	Feb, 8 2019
Custodial Worker (Custodial)	OCEANA NAVAL AIR STATION, VIRGINIA	Feb, 8 2019
CYP Food Service Worker	KITTERY, MAINE	Feb, 8 2019
Laundry Worker - NGIS	BOLLING AFB, DISTRICT OF COLUMBIA	Feb, 8 2019
CYP Operations Clerk	MANAMA, BAHRAIN	Feb, 8 2019
Custodial Worker (Housekeeping)	OCEANA NAVAL AIR STATION, VIRGINIA	Feb, 9 2019

NAF Employment Benefits

Who Can Receive NAF Employment Benefits?

NAF positions are classified as either "flexible" or "regular." Flexible employees have work schedules that depend on the needs of the activity. These employees may work a minimum of zero hours to a maximum of 40 hours per week, and do not receive benefits. Regular employees work between 20 and 40 hours a week depending on position requirements, and are entitled to receive benefits.

Benefits and Privileges:

All NAF employees are encouraged to enjoy the use of NAF facilities and take advantage of a variety of employee benefits. (May vary from base to base.) Facilities/benefits include:

- Exchanges
- Lodging & Dining Clubs
- Childcare Facilities
- Movie Theaters & Parks
- Swimming Pools & Fitness Centers
- Golf Courses
- Bowling Centers
- Marinas & Ocean Fishing
- Libraries
- Hobby Shops
- Discount Tickets to your favorite places and Leisure Travel Deals
- Flexible Schedules
- Training Opportunities
- Tuition Assistance at applicable commands
- Balance of Work & Family Life
- Employee Assistance Program (EAP)
- Paid Holidays
- Financial Wellness Program

All of this in a secure, fast-paced, professional, family-oriented working environment.

Employee Benefits Available to All Regular Full-Time and Regular Part-Time Civilian NAF Employees:

- Medical and Dental
- Life Insurance
- Optional and Dependent Life Insurance
- Accidental Death and Dismemberment
- 401(k) Savings Plan
- Group Retirement Plan
- Family Friendly Leave Program
- Flexible Spending Account
- Long-Term Care
- Short-Term Disability
- Leave (Sick & Vacation)

For Employees and Retirees

The DOD implemented the Health Benefits Program (HBP) on January 1, 2000. It provides comprehensive benefits which include hospitalization, prescription drugs, medical, surgical, preventive, mental health, substance abuse, vision, and dental care.

U.S. Army MWR NAF Position Benefits: https://www.armymwr.com/naf-benefits.aspx

Derived Preference

Derived Preference is a method by which you, as the spouse, widow/widower, or mother of a veteran may be eligible to claim veterans' preference when your veteran is unable to use it. You will be given XP Preference (10 points) in appointment if you meet the eligibility criteria.

Both a mother and a spouse (including widow or widower) may be entitled to preference on the basis of the same veteran's service if they both meet the requirements. However, neither may receive preference if the veteran is living and is qualified for federal employment.

Spouses are eligible when your veteran has a service-connected disability and has been unable to qualify for any position in the civil service.

Widows/Widowers are eligible if you did not divorce your veteran spouse, have not remarried, or the remarriage was annulled, and the veteran:

- ✪ served during a war or during the period April 28, 1952, through July 1, 1955, or in a campaign or expedition for which a campaign medal has been authorized; OR
- ✪ died while on active duty that included service described immediately above under conditions that would not have been the basis for other than an honorable or general discharge.

Mothers of deceased veterans are eligible when your son or daughter died under honorable conditions while on active duty during a war or in a campaign or expedition for which a campaign medal has been authorized. Additionally, you must:

- ✪ be or have been married to the father of your veteran; AND
- ✪ live with a permanently disabled husband; OR
- ✪ be widowed, divorced, or separated from the veteran's father and have not remarried; OR
- ✪ if remarried be widowed, divorced, or legally separated from your husband at the time you claim derived preference.

The SF-15 form is required to utilize the 10-Point Derived Preference hiring authority (https://www.opm.gov/Forms/pdf_fill/SF15.pdf)

Mothers of disabled veterans are eligible if your son or daughter was separated with an honorable or general discharge from active duty, including training service in the Reserves or National Guard, and is permanently and totally disabled from a service-connected injury or illness. Additionally, you must:

- ✪ be or have been married to the father of your veteran; AND
- ✪ live with a permanently disabled husband; OR
- ✪ be widowed, divorced, or separated from the veteran's father and have not remarried; OR
- ✪ if remarried, be widowed, divorced, or legally separated from your husband at the time you claim derived preference.

Source: https://www.fedshirevets.gov/job/familypref/index.aspx

Successful Application with Derived Preference: Results Email From DOD

---------- Forwarded message ----------
From: **Vacancy ID: 1734946** <usastaffingoffice@opm.gov>
Date: Mon, Aug 8, 2016 at 3:26 PM
Subject: Notification Letter Vacancy ID: 1734946
TO: susanne

DOJ - HEADQUARTERS COMPONENTS
JUSTICE MANAGEMENT DIVISION
145 N STREET NE SUITE 9W 300
WASHINGTON DC 20530

Dear SUSANNE JAMES,

This refers to the application you recently submitted to this office for the position below:

Position Title: Administrative Specialist
Promotion Potential: 09
Vacancy ID: 1734946
Agency: Offices, Boards and Divisions
Considered For: COMMUNITY RELATIONS SERVICES
Duty Location: Washington DC, DC

We have reviewed your application and found you qualified for the position listed above. ***Your name has been referred to the employing agency for consideration.***

Program S (Priority Placement Program for Spouses)

The Department of Defense (DOD) Priority Placement Program (PPP) is a DOD-wide program that provides referrals and priority when applying for Department of Defense civilian jobs. Military spouses may also participate in the PPP under Program S, also known as PPP-S. Contact the Civilian Human Resources Officer on your installation for assistance with getting on the PPP-S Registry.

How it Works

STEP**01** Register for the PPP, which is a separate database from USAJOBS.

STEP**02** HR will let you know you are matched to a position on USAJOBS. Or you can search for matching jobs yourself.

STEP**03** Apply in USAJOBS.

STEP**04** If Best Qualified, you may receive priority during the application process.

Who Qualifies for Program S?

Everyone who qualifies for E.O. 13473 (see Part 1)

UPCOMING CHANGES: As of the printing of this edition, PPP is undergoing changes that may affect military spouses' eligibility to be placed on the registry in the future.

Match Your Federal Resume for Program S

Match Your Resume to the PPP Handbook Chapter 10 Option Codes

A human resources specialist will be reviewing your resume and scoring it in terms of the potential grade level, occupational series, and Program S option codes (knowledge, skills and abilities) that your resume represents. Your resume is critical to the success of your Program S registration score and the possible matches to USAJOBS positions.40 hours a week depending on position requirements, and are entitled to receive benefits.

Where can I find the Program S Option Codes?

PPP Handbook Chapter 10 is available on the Resume Place website at www.resume-place.com (click on Military Spouses).

You can qualify for up to 10 Option Codes per job series.

The more Option Codes you qualify for, the more matches you could receive!

CHAPTER 10

OPTION CODES

A. PURPOSE

The purpose of this Chapter is to explain the proper use of option codes, which are used in registration to more specifically define qualifications and in requisitioning to clarify job requirements.

B. PROCEDURAL REQUIREMENTS

Except for the six generic options (see B.6., below) and the NOA option code (see B.2. below), option codes may be used only with the specific occupational series under which they are listed in Appendix A.

1. The registration format will accommodate up to 10 option codes per skill line. Decisions as to which options, if any, may be used, are based solely on a registrant's qualifications. An option code should never be entered more than once for the same occupational series.

Sample Program S Registration

Remember, more option codes and grade levels on your Program S registration will help you match more job announcements in the DOD announcement database.

If you feel that you should be matched to more option codes, occupational series, or grades, improve your resume and return.

```
                                              REGISTRATION
RSN:58B11          ACTY:250A        LACT: 238A      NAME:                        EMAIL:
EDIPI: 1                            COMP DATA: HRO_ID
HRO-POC:        , JESSICA     HRO-PHONE:215-697-      PROGRAM: S    PRIORITY: S
HRO DSN PHONE:442-0358        HRO FAX: 215-697-       HRO DSN FAX: 442-0439
HRO EMAIL:JESSICA          @NAVY.MIL
HRO EMAIL2:HRSCNE_PPP-Team@navy.mil

MISC CODE: JM                 ORIGINATE: 2019/01/11    IN:          OUT:
ACT:            PG:           SER:   GR:              ACTY:        REQ:          CA:
ADDRESS:                            COMPONENT:N
CITY:                         STATE: MD                            SEPARATION DATE:
ZIP:                          TELEPHONE:                           RELEASE DATE:
POSITION: GS 0343 11               JOB TITLE: PROGRAM MANAGER
SALARY:           SECURITY CLEARANCE: N        TENURE GROUP:            SCD:

OVERSEAS COUNTRY:             RETURN RIGHTS: N      RETURN RIGHTS AK-HI-RQ-GQ:
RETAINED GRADE:          N    SEASONAL:              N
APPOINTMENT ELIG:        H    SUPERVISORY:           Y
                             SUPERVISORY PROBATION:  N
EXCEPTED SERVICE:       NE    DEFENSE ACQUISITION CORPS:  N
VSIP:                         DOD OVERSEAS:          N
TEMPORARY:              N     RESERVE TECHNICIAN:    N
PART TIME:              N     BASE CLOSURE:          N
INTERMITTENT:          N      ROTATING SHIFTS:       N
WOUNDED WARRIOR:
EDUCATION:5                   DEGREE:M               MAJOR:LEAD. OF HEALTHCARE
```

-- EXPERIENCE --	FROM	TO	TITLE
	201609	201706	GRADUATE STUDENT (16HR/WK)
	201508	201607	PROGRAM MANAGER CAREER COACH
	201402	201706	EMPLOYMENT SERVICES & TRNG COOR
	200911	201302	FAMILY READINESS OFFICER
	200907	201306	FAMILY READINESS ASST-VOLUNTEER

-- SKILLS --	PG	SER	HI	LO	EX	HD
	GS	0301	11	09	05	
Options:	HCA LOA FSP ANA TRB MLP REC PER MWR PRC					
	GS	0340	11	09	05	
Options:	MWR PHR					
	GS	0343	11	09	05	
Options:	HCA MBR MAL PHR STP TEV REC					
	GS	1101	11	09	05	
Options:	MKT REK					
	GS	1712	11	09	05	
Options:	HEB LOA MIT					

```
AWARDS:N
MISC QUALS:
ZONE:
REGION:
STATES:
COMPONENT:
COMMUTING AREA ONLY: Y
ACTIVITIES: 168A 177A 200A 201A 204A 207A 207C 231A 232D 232E 238A 239A 253A 276A 279A 284B 297B
COUNTRIES:
APPROVING OFFICIAL:
```

Set Up Your Program S Meeting

To find the Program S HRO at your installation, ask your employment readiness or transition service counselors for the name of the current HRO specialist who provides Program S registration. Make your appointment to talk to or meet your HRO representative. It might take a few phone calls or emails, but persevere in making this appointment. Your registration meeting could take up to two hours!

What to Bring: Bring a copy of your resume and other application documents.

During your appointment:

- You will learn about Program S.
- Expect to go through the three-page, 31-question Program S registration/counseling checklist. Initial each item after being counseled.
- HRO will put you into the PPP-S system.
- HRO will decide which occupational series, Option Codes, and grade levels for which your resume will be considered.
- If you previously worked for DOD, your grade level may not be higher than what you previously held. If you haven't, your grade will be determined by your employment history and education.
- You will receive a PPP registration form. Don't leave without it.
- The registration form will let you know which positions you can be matched to.

PPP Match Notification

This is a very exciting email!

You could receive an email from a human resources specialist telling you that you are MATCHED for a specific position. This is NOT a job offer, but there is a MATCH.

- Registering HRO notifies you if you are matched or selected.
- To accept a Program S position you MUST be in the position before you move to your next PCS location.
- You can only receive one continuing (permanent) position job offer per PCS.
- If you reject this offer, you cannot be offered another one.
- You may receive unlimited appointments to non-continuing positions.

Sample Match Email—PLEASE NOTE: This is NOT a job offer.

I am contacting you because it is my understanding that you are registered in the Priority Placement Program (PPP) (Program S-Military Spouse). Your registration was a potential match to a Social Services Assistant, GS-0186-08, position at Schofield Barracks, HI. During your preliminary PPP consultation, you should have been told that you are required to have a current resume in Application Manager. When a registrant matches against a PPP requisition, the registrant will be contacted and directed to submit an application package through USAJOBS (http://www.usajobs.gov/) including responses to the questionnaire associated with the recruitment action. If it is not feasible for you to complete the application process online, you may provide a completed 1203FX via whatever means is available (e.g., scan and email, fax, provide in person).

The Social Services Assistant announcement (Announcement # NCMD156124361346945) is scheduled to open on Tuesday, March 10, 2015 and will close on Thursday, March 12, 2015. It is your responsibility to apply for this position. According to Chapter 14, Section C.4.b. of the DOD PPP Operations Manual, spouses who decline to participate in established competitive recruitment procedures, such as submitting resumes or responding to assessment questionnaires, will lose their eligibility for continued registration in the Military Spouse Program.

Sample Match Email

As a result of your Priority Placement Program (PPP) registration, you have been identified as a match for an Information Referral & Follow Up Program Manager position, GS-0101-09 position at USAG-HI, IMCOM, Directorate of Morale Welfare & Recreation, Army Community Services Division on Oahu Island, HI. The vacancy announcement is already closed, but you are currently showing as an applicant who has applied for this vacancy already; therefore, you are not required to apply.

Get Best Qualified on PPP-S

In order for your Program S and USAJOBS application to MATCH, you must be Best Qualified for the position. Be sure to score the application Questionnaire the highest possible, so that the HR specialist can see a MATCH between your resume and one of the Program S job announcements. It will be your number one goal to get Best Qualified and/or Referred for positions.

What Happens if I Get Best Qualified?

- If you are found "BEST QUALIFIED," your resume will move into the selection pool and all other competitive applicants will be blocked (non-competitive applicants do not get blocked).

- Management may choose to select a non-competitive applicant or an applicant from an alternative recruitment source (such as VRA, Schedule A person with disabilities) rather than a Program S spouse.

- A higher priority candidate may be selected instead. Priority 1 and 2 registrants (e.g., DOD civilian employees adversely affected by base closure, realignment, or reduction-in-force) get selected first, then Priority S (Program S).

- If there is more than one Priority S applicant, the selecting official may select either.

- If there are no Priority 1 or 2 candidates, a Program S spouse will be selected UNLESS the selecting official decides to select from within the organization.

- Veterans' preference does not apply.

Ideas for Standing Out With a MATCH Email from HRO

- Upload letters of reference from previous employers.
- Strategically volunteer at organizations where you wish to work.
- When reporting to the installation, introduce yourself to organizations where you wish to work.
- If you are a current federal employee, see if your current manager will contact his or her counterpart about your impending arrival.

Interviews

If the results of interviews are not factored into rating and ranking, interviews are NOT allowed. However, if personal interviews are being used as an integral part of the process, managers may choose to interview "Best Qualified" spouses.

So, for PPP-S and USAJOBS, your resume really must speak for you!

PART 04
Exercises: It's Your Turn!

"I just wasn't sure where to start with my federal job search and how to start writing my federal resume."

It's Your Turn: Start Your Military Spouse Job Block

PCS History (Locations and Dates):

See sample PCS histories: Nicole (page 47), Bobbi (59), Jan (70), Ann (80) Natalie (89), Jennifer (97)

Summary of Skills (what skills did you gain as a military spouse?):

See sample skill summaries: Nicole (page 47), Bobbi (59), Jan (70), Ann (80) Natalie (89), Jennifer (97)

Finding Keywords in Job Announcements

Below are several sample job announcements. We identified the keywords from the specialized experience section. On the next page, it's your turn to identify the keywords.

CONTACT REPRESENTATIVE, GS-0962-05/07
(Customer Services Representative)

GS-5: 52 weeks of full-time specialized experience equivalent to the GS-4 level in the Federal Service performing all or most of the following tasks: 1) Applying laws, regulations policies or procedures to provide assistance preparing forms or documents; 2) Answering questions from members of the public or their representatives to obtain or provide information; 3) Using a computer to reconcile discrepancies or entering data; and 4) responding to written inquiries and drafting a variety of other written products.

Keywords

- ✪ RESEARCH AND ANALYZE REGULATORY SOURCES
- ✪ ANSWER QUESTIONS AND EXPLAIN RIGHTS AND REGULATIONS
- ✪ UTILIZE COMPUTERS TO RECONCILE DISCREPANCIES
- ✪ ENTER DATA INTO DATABASES
- ✪ RESPOND TO INQUIRIES CONCERNING PROGRAM REQUIREMENTS

INVENTORY MANAGEMENT SPECIALIST, GS 2010-07

Specialized Experience: You must have one year of specialized experience equivalent to at least the next lower grade GS-6 for the occupation in the organization. Examples of specialized experience would typically include, but are not limited to:

Determines the means and methods to resolve issues and improve operations.
Administers an expendable inventory management program.
Coordinates with property managers for disposal of surplus or excess supplies.

Keywords

- ✪ INVENTORY MANAGEMENT ADMINISTRATION
- ✪ COORDINATE WITH CUSTOMERS ON ORDERS AND DEDLINES
- ✪ RESOLVE ISSUES AND IMPROVE OPERATIONS
- ✪ CUSTOMER SERVICES
- ✪ FLEXIBILITY AND PROBLEM-SOLVING

It's Your Turn: Finding Keywords

Find the keywords from the specialized experience section

Administrative Assistant, DHS, TSA, Pay Band SV-#

Qualifications

To qualify at the SV-E Pay Band, (equivalent to GS-7/8) you must have one year of specialized experience equivalent to the SV-D or GS-6 in the Federal service or equivalent experience in the private sector. **Specialized experience** is defined as experience that has equipped you with the particular knowledge, skills, and abilities required to successfully perform the duties of this position. Such experience includes providing payroll support, **AND** applying knowledge of at least two (2) of the following:

- Identifying payroll issues related to time and attendance, pay, and leave;
- Interacting with staff to exchange information;
- Preparing, reviewing and modifying documents, letters, memos or reports using word processing software;
- Compiling, tracking and analyzing data;
- Developing charts and tables for reports and briefings; **OR**
- Coordinating travel and preparing travel orders and vouchers;

This definition of specialized experience is typical of work performed at the next lower grade/level position in the federal service (GS-05).

List the keywords below:

- ☆ _____
- ☆ _____
- ☆ _____
- ☆ _____
- ☆ _____

How to Stand Out with Accomplishments

STEP01
Make a Top Ten List of you accomplishments.

STEP02
Write compelling stories about each accomplishment using CCAR (Context | Challenge | Action | Result).

STEP03
Shorten them to add to your resume.

STEP04
Practice telling them out loud for the Behavior-Based Interview.

What is CCAR?

We use what we call the CCAR model to tell an accomplishment story. It's super easy once you understand it. Kathryn walks Jan through the CCAR method about her Sesame Street room story (See Jan's case study in Part 2).

⭐ CONTEXT

Kathryn: Let's talk about your accomplishment of opening the very first Sesame Room in Europe. That sounds like an interesting story! Tell me a little bit of background about this story.

Jan: I was serving as the ACS Director at the U.S. Army Garrison in Wiesbaden, and I wanted to help the New Parent Support Program host classes and play groups for parents with infants and toddlers.

⭐ CHALLENGE

Kathryn: What was the problem?

Jan: They did not have a location for an office or to host the events.

⭐ ACTION

Kathryn: Wow, that was a big problem! So what did you do?

Jan: I found a vacant three-bedroom apartment in one of our buildings. I also saw the opportunity to apply to create Sesame Rooms on military installations. I submitted a proposal to Sesame Street and had our team clean and prepare the three-bedroom apartment for use as an office space and play area.

⭐ RESULT

Kathryn: What happened because of your actions?

Jan: We were awarded a $5,000 Sesame Room Make Over! The Garrison Commander, media, and 50 guests attended the grand opening of our room and enjoyed touring the facility with new paint, carpets, toys, educational materials, and other items. The room was the first of its kind in Europe.

It's Your Turn: Write Your Accomplishment Story

Context:

_____

_____

_____

_____

_____

Challenge:

_____

_____

_____

_____

_____

Action:

_____

_____

_____

_____

_____

Result:

_____

_____

_____

_____

_____

About the Author:
Kathryn Troutman

1. Founder, President, and Manager of The Resume Place®, the first federal job search consulting and federal resume writing service in the world, and the producer of www.resume-place.com, the first website devoted to federal resume writing.

2. Pioneer designer of the federal resume format in 1995 with the publication of the leading resource for federal human resources and jobseekers worldwide—the *Federal Resume Guidebook*, now in its sixth edition and the #2 resume book on the internet.

3. Developer of the Certified Federal Job Search Trainer®/Certified Federal Career Coach® train-the-trainer program in 2002. Licensing *Ten Steps to a Federal Job*®, a curriculum and turnkey training program taught by more than 5,000 Certified Federal Job Search Trainers® (CFJST) around the world. Recommended by military services for transition and employment readiness counselors around the world.

4. Authored the first-ever book for military spouses and Federal job search, *The Stars Are Lined Up for Military Spouses*, 2017. Authored and published the second edition with the FIRST-EVER Military Spouse Federal Resume with PCS Military Spouse Career History featured in the resume.

5. Author of numerous federal career publications (in addition to the *Federal Resume Guidebook* mentioned above):

The *Military to Federal Career Guide* is the first book for military personnel and is now in its second edition, featuring veteran federal resumes. Troutman recognized the need for returning military personnel from Iraq, Afghanistan, and Kosovo to have a resource available to them in their searches for government jobs.

Ten Steps to a Federal Job was published two months after 9/11 and was written for private industry jobseekers seeking first-time positions in the federal government, where they could contribute to our nation's security. Now in its third edition.

The *Jobseeker's Guide* started initially as the companion course handout to the Ten Steps book, but captured its own following when it became the handout text used by over 200 military installations throughout the world for transitioning military and family members. Now in its eighth edition.

With the looming human capital crisis and baby boomers retiring in government, the *Student's Federal Career Guide* was co-authored with Kathryn's daughter and MPP graduate, Emily Troutman, and is the first book for students pursuing a federal job. Now in its third edition, including the latest information on the changing structure of student programs.

Training Resources and Help for Military Spouses

Military Spouse Federal Resume Writing and Coaching

The Resume Place, Inc. Federal Resume Writing services for Military Spouses. Professional consulting services, writing, editing, coaching services for military spouses to navigate Program S and USAJOBS applications. Federal Career Consulting on USAJOBS announcement selection and total federal job search services.

To see services and information: www.resume-place.com

Licensed Curriculum and Certification Training

This book and the Stars are Lined Up for Military Spouses Slide Deck are part of the Certified Federal Job Search Trainer® and Certified Federal Career Coach® curriculum. Get certified and Licensed to teach Ten Steps to a Federal Job® and The Stars are Lined Up for Military Spouses at your military installation.

More information: www.resume-place.com

Half-Day Workshop

The Stars Are Lined Up for Military Spouses is a 1/2 day course that is available to be taught at government agencies and military bases worldwide. The course is listed on the GSA Schedule and is available for your military base.

More information and requests for quotes:
Kathryn Troutman, kathryn@resume-place.com

RESUME PLACE

BUILDING CAREERS IN THE US GOVERNMENT

Publications by the Resume Place, Inc.

Order online at www.resume-place.com | Bulk Orders: (888) 480 8265
FREE SHIPPING of bulk orders in the domestic US and APO
E-books available for immediate download at www.resume-place.com

Jobseeker's Guide, 8th Edition—Military to Federal Career Transition Resource. Workbook and guide for the Ten Steps to a Federal Job® training curriculum. Federal job search strategies for first-time jobseekers who are separating military and family members. *$18.95. $8 ea for 50+ books + shipping.*

The Stars Are Lined Up for Military Spouses, 2nd Edition—Key book to assist military spouses with navigating USAJOBS and the complex federal job process. Covers four ways to land the major kinds of federal positions for military spouses. *$14.95. $8 ea for 50+ books + shipping.*

Federal Resume Guidebook, 6th Edition—Now the #2 Resume Book in America! The ultimate guide in federal resume and KSA writing. Easy to use as a template for writing. Specialty occupational series chapters. *$15.95. $10 ea for 50+ books + shipping.*

The **New SES Application, 2nd Edition** breaks down this complex application process into a step-by-step guide based on a popular workshop taught for over 10 years. Updated with SES info to help you navigate hiring reforms currently impacting the Senior Executive Service. *$21.95. Bulk rates available.*

Student's Federal Career Guide, 3rd Edition takes the 2013 IndieFab Gold Winner for Career Books! Outstanding book for jobseekers who are just getting out of college and whose education will help the applicant get qualified for a position. 20 samples of recent graduate resumes with emphasis on college degrees, courses, major papers, internships, and relevant work experiences. *$9.95. Available in PDF.*

Creating Your First Resume is a book used at high school and technical school programs nationwide. The new edition boasts brand new resume samples that represent the push toward STEM technical programs to provide training and certifications for high school students. *$12.95. $5 ea for 50+ books + shipping.*

Federal Resume Database—This online resource contains more than 110 resume samples and federal job search resources from the current Resume Place publications. Sample resumes are available in Word & PDF format for easy reading and editing. *Individual and Agency / Base Licenses available*